COMMUNICATION
FOR ALL

Philip Lee

editor

COMMUNICATION FOR ALL

New World Information and Communication Order

Maryknoll, New York 10545

The Catholic Foreign Mission Society of America (Maryknoll) recruits and trains people for overseas missionary service. Through Orbis Books Maryknoll aims to foster the international dialogue that is essential to mission. The books published, however, reflect the opinions of their authors and are not meant to represent the official position of the society.

First published as *Communication for All: The Church and The New World Information and Communication Order* by Satprakashan Sanchar Kendra, Indore 452 001, Madhya Pradesh, India, in association with Orbis Books, Maryknoll, NY 10545, and Daystar Press, P. O. Box 1261, Ibadan, Nigeria. Copyright © 1985 by World Association for Christian Communication, 122 King's Road, London SW3, England.

This trade edition published, with slight revisions, in 1986 by Orbis Books.

Manufactured in the United States of America
All rights reserved.

Library of Congress Cataloging-in-Publication Data

Communication for all.

   Bibliography: p.
   1. Communication, International.   2. Communication—International cooperation.   3. Communication—Religious aspects—Christianity.   4. Women in communication.
I. Lee, Philip.
P96.I5C66   1986   001.51   86-5134
ISBN 0-88344-246-9 (pbk.)

Contents

Foreword *by Michael Traber*   ix
    Communication: A Human Right   x
    Participation and Democratization   xi
   Notes   xiii

CHAPTER ONE   1
Johan Galtung
Social Communication and Global Problems
    The Nature of Social Communication   3
      News Communication as a Function of Western Social Cosmology   7
      Division of Space   7
      Sources of Negativism   7
      Fragmentation of Reality and Knowledge   8
      Nature Subordinated   8
      Individualism and Competition   8
      The New(s) God   9
      Some Consequences   9
    Toward a New International Information/Communication Order?   10
    Conclusion: Toward a New and Global Journalism   14
    Notes   15

CHAPTER TWO   17
Herbert I. Schiller
Strengths and Weaknesses of the New International Information Empire
    The Current Global State of Production and Sale of Cultural Goods and Services   18
    New Information Technologies and NWICO   20
    TNC Interests in the International Politicol-Legal Arena   25
    Conclusion: Transnational Ideology and Preservation of the Human Community   29
    Notes   30

CHAPTER THREE   33
Margaret Gallagher
Women and NWICO
    Women's Status and Socio-Economic Definitions   34

Women's Status and the Role of Information   35
Communicating the Status of Women   37
Women's Status and Communication Systems: Structural
    Relationships   38
    Global Issues   39
    National Issues   43
    Women: Central and Peripheral to Communication and Change   47
An Issue in Its Own Right   51
Women and the Composition of Knowledge, Information, and
    Communication   51
Bibliographic References   53

CHAPTER FOUR   57
Paul A. V. Ansah
African Responses to the NWICO Debate
Information and the African State   59
The Pan-African News Agency (PANA)   60
NWICO and Community Media   63
NWICO and the Training of Media Personnel   65
Conclusions   67
Notes   69

CHAPTER FIVE   70
Washington Uranga
NWICO: New World Information and Communication Order
Introduction   70
Understanding the Problem of Communication Today   71
    Communication as a Global Phenomenon   72
    Transnationalization and World Crisis   74
    The Culture Industry   76
    Cultural Invasion   78
    Communication and Crosscultural Domination   80
NWICO: A Proposal for Change   82
    Three Stages in the NWICO Debate   82
    The Most Important Need: Democratization of Communication   84
    Development and Communication   86
    Participants in Democratic Communication   88
    Education and Communication   89
    Alternative Communication: An Integral Part of Social Change
        and Human Development   90
Church and Communication: Pastoral Responses   95
    Self-Defense   96
    Apostolic Conquest   96
    Critical Training   96
    Group Communication   97
    Communication for Liberation   98

Proposals for Action   99
   Understanding Communication as an Inseparable Part of the Social Process   99
   Working for Cultural Creativity   100
   Promoting Networks of Alternative Communication   100
   Educating for Communication   101
   Reviewing Communication by and in the Church   102
Notes   102

CHAPTER SIX   105
Robert A. White
Christians Building a New Order of Communication
Questions, Options, Decisions   106
   Historical Trend Toward Public Responsibility for the Media   109
   Origin of the NWICO Debate   109
   Development of the Principle of the Right to Communicate   111
   Media Decentralization and Control   113
   Participatory Communication   113
   Education for Participatory Communication   114
   Questioning Authoritarian Models in the Science of Communication   115
How Can Christian Communicators Contribute to NWICO?   115

CHAPTER SEVEN   118
Gaston Roberge
Communication and the Church in India
Evangelization, Communication, Development   119
The Need for Healthy Theory   122
The Indian Church and NWICO   123
The Need for Pragmatic Research   125
The Need for Professionalism   126
The Need for Concern for Communication Issues   127
The Need to Clarify the Attitude of the Church toward Communication Technology   128
Notes   129

CHAPTER EIGHT   131
Colleen Roach
Select Annotated Bibliography on a New World Information and Communication Order (NWICO)
Books and Pamphlets on NWICO   131
Books and Pamphlets on Related Aspects of NWICO   135
Documents, Periodicals, Articles   147
Bibliographies   154

Contributors   157

Foreword

The industrialized countries of the North have never fully grasped the implications of what has been called the process of decolonization. This applies equally to the ex-colonial powers of Britain and France and to the present day superpowers, the USA and the Soviet Union. The attainment of sovereign independence by more than fifty nations in the second half of this century was seen as the culmination and thus the end of a process by the North. The countries of the South, however, considered independence as the starting point for the long, and once again difficult, process of taking charge of their own destiny. For political independence to be meaningful, economic sovereignty had to follow. A further step on the road toward complete decolonization was the redevelopment of the various cultures into which serious inroads had been made by the colonial masters, particularly in Africa. The economic and cultural emancipation called for a third process, namely that of the decolonization of the information systems, or the need for a new information order.

In the movement leading towards decolonization, the United Nations organizations played a leading part. The UN and its specialized agencies not only provided a platform for the representatives of the South, but also acted as think-tanks from which ideas for a new global order were proposed. The demand for economic decolonization led to the call for a "New International Economic Order" (NIEO), which was published as a major document in 1975. This led to the appointment of the Brandt Commission and its report "North-South: A Program for Survival" (1980). In 1976 the nonaligned countries staked out their demand in UNESCO for a "New International Information Order" (NIIO), and this was followed by the appointment of the MacBride Commission in December 1977. The main issues with which the International Commission for the Study of Communication Problems (chaired by the Irish statesman Sean MacBride) was concerned can be summarized as follows:

• The continuing and increasing dependence of the Third World countries on the rich industrialized countries for nearly all of their communication equipment, technology, skills, and software.
• The increasing integration of the poor countries into a system dominated by multinational corporations which for the most part have private profit as their main goal.
• Through such integration, the progressive dilution of indigenous cultures.
• The reduction of information from being a basic right to being a commodity for sale.
• The overwhelming imbalance in the flow of news, television programs, films,

magazines, books and other cultural software between the rich and poor countries, whereby the rich countries overwhelmed the poor with alien models and values, making national development goals almost impossible to realize.
- The slanting of news and misreportage of Third World events by the powerful agencies based in the rich world so that the images of poor countries, their cultures, struggles, and development efforts were often a gross caricature of the reality.
- The unfair advantages enjoyed by the rich countries in international institutions in the allocation of frequencies in the electromagnetic spectrum.
- The threat to the sovereignty of nations as a result of developments in satellite broadcasting technology.
- The almost irreversible concentration of power in the hands of the rich countries achieved through computer data banks and global computer networks owned and managed by multinational corporations primarily to their commercial advantage.

The debate centered on a clear North-South, First World-Third World, or rich versus poor confrontation. The poor countries were charging the rich with exercising monopoly, manipulation, domination, misrepresentation and distortion in the area of international information. But the MacBride Commission put the issues into a wider context. In his preface to the Commission's Report, Sean MacBride wrote: "Ours is not simply a report on the collection and dissemination of news, or on the mass media. . . . We have been involved in a wider historical, political, and sociological perspective . . . concentration on information had to be broadened to include all aspects of communication, considered in an overall social, economic" and political context. The recommendations of the MacBride report (1980) are of course still concerned with the problems of cultural decolonization. But the call for a New World Information and Communication Order (NWICO) has much broader implications.

Communication: A Human Right

The first and most important problem that NWICO raises is that of communication as a basic human right. Human rights spring from human needs, and human life apparently depends on communication. Cut off from it, persons cannot develop or attain their full potential. To be fully human, they must communicate. Communication, however, is not just an individual but also a social necessity. Without communication there can be no real community. It is the link between individuals who constitute a community, and the link between communities in the formation of a larger whole—a metropolis, a province, a nation. "Societies as a whole cannot survive today if they are not properly informed about political affairs, international and local events."[1]

If a human right is so essential that its denial amounts to an offense against the very nature of personhood—such as the right to life, the right to liberty, the right to religious belief, or in this case the right to communicate—it is called a fundamental human right. Whereas some other rights—freedom of speech, freedom of the press, or freedom of association—may be limited in special circumstances, a fundamental human right, such as communication, must always be upheld because it is necessary for the proper functioning and development of human beings and the social environment they need.[2]

The right to communicate has, of course, its counterpart in the right of others not to have their personal freedom violated. Communication must go hand in hand with responsibility, which means:

> Primarily a concern for truth and the legitimate use of the power it conveys.... The freedom of a citizen or social group to have access to [public] communication, both as recipient and as contributor, cannot be compared to the freedom of an investor to derive profit from the media. One protects a fundamental human right, the other permits the commercialization of a social need.[3]

In our age of mass communication, public communication has become more and more commercialized and monopolized. The individual human rights to "seek, receive, and impart information and ideas" have in effect been diminished because of increasing monopolization in the dissemination of information and entertainment to huge and passive audiences.

The rights of nations to participate in a multidirectional flow of information on the basis of equality was one of the starting points in the demand for a new information order, which was mainly the concern of nonaligned nations (mostly the developing countries of the South). It was their way of saying no to their increasing integration into the corporate village of global communication dominated by the North, saying no to the "freedom" of private corporations to infringe on the rights of nation-states:

> The right to communicate, in a single phrase, encapsulates most of the aspirations of the NWICO. When flesh is put on the bare bones of this concept, the ideal world where the right to communicate is recognized and implemented will look very like a world in which the new order of information and communication has been established.[4]

Participation and Democratization

Another NWICO cornerstone is the demand for participatory and democratic communication:

> Over fifty years experience of the mass media—press, film, radio, and television—have conditioned us, both at the national and international levels, to a single kind of information flow, which we have come to accept as normal and indeed as the only possible kind: a vertical, one-way flow from the top downward of non-diversified anonymous messages, produced by a few and addressed to all. That is not communication.

Confronted by this problem, however, our "mass media mentality" reacts only by stepping up the vertical flow, increasing everywhere the number of newspapers, radio and television receivers, and cinemas, especially in developing countries, without recognizing that it is the very vertical nature of the flow which is at issue.[5]

These words were written by Jean d'Arcy who, after a lifetime of broadcasting in France, called upon his hearers to gather together in neighborhoods and small communities to establish their right to communication by setting up community radio systems and grass-roots newspapers—thus stemming the vertical flow.

Indeed, communication systems organized on vertical lines—with the flow from top to bottom, from the center to the periphery, from the few to the many, from the information-rich to the information-poor—do not fully meet the needs of individuals and society. A horizontal flow of information is required both within and between nations so that genuine communication can take place.

Communication today is increasingly seen as a process through which the exchange and sharing of meaning is made possible, and by which social relationships and, as a result, social institutions are created and maintained. It is a two-way process, interactive by its very nature. This concept of communication demands participation.

On the local and national level this means promoting low-cost media, and facilitating and encouraging individuals and groups to participate. It also calls for the creation of interactive media. The technological developments of recent years have opened up possibilities for more flexible use, for "talk back" and participation for both individuals and groups.

Participation will eventually demand a change in the rules of journalism according to which the powerful, rich, and glamorous occupy center stage, to the exclusion of ordinary men and women. How can they participate if these rules, maintained in the name of "professionalism," imply that their voices do not deserve to be heard unless they do something bizarre or become the victims of crime or accident?

On the international level, countries now on the receiving end of the information and entertainment industries should be assisted to harness their own resources to manufacture equipment and to produce local programming so that an exchange between nations is possible. The availability of adequate facilities and their equitable distribution between and within societies are NWICO goals, "which are so basic that solutions cannot be delayed."[6]

Both the call for the promulgation and implementation of communication as a fundamental human right and the demand for more participatory and more democratic communication must be seen in the light of justice, with which the churches could and should identify. "Justice demands the establishment of minimum levels of participation by all persons in the life of the human community," was how the Catholic Bishops' Conference of the U.S.A. put it;

and "the most urgent demand of justice" was to overcome "patterns of marginalization and powerlessness." Social institutions must grant every person "the ability to participate actively in the economic, political, and cultural life of the community."⁷ There are few areas of life and few social institutions in which popular participation is so weak (or indeed nonexistent) as it is in public communication, and this despite the fact that communication affects the lives of all.

Another issue is that of effectiveness. As more persons become involved in the process of communication, it will become more effective. Change in personal attitudes and behavior seems to be most favored by the process of group communication. Groups then assume communication power and direct it toward certain goals or values. This has been done admirably by thousands of Christian base communities in Latin America and elsewhere. It is partly through this process of *comunicación popular* that new life and vigor has come to those Christian communities, in contrast to the fossilization of much of established church life in the North.

If there is a single common denominator among the contributions to this book it is the call for communication power on the grass-roots level. Such communication can become an agent for change in religious life, socio-economic development, and in the struggle for human rights. "Self-reliance, cultural identity, freedom, independence, respect for human dignity, mutual aid, participation in the reshaping of the environment—these are some of the nonmaterial aspirations which all seek through communication."⁸ Surely this is where the churches must meet the new world information and communication order.

Michael Traber,
World Association for Christian Communication, London

NOTES

1. UNESCO, *Many Voices, One World,* Paris, 1980, p. 14. This report commissioned by UNESCO, is commonly called the MacBride Report. Sean MacBride, the Irish international statesman, presided over the 16-member International Commission for the Study of Communication Problems.

2. See Desmond Fisher, "From Concept to Action," in D. Fisher and L. S. Harms, *The Right to Communicate: A New Human Right,* Dublin, Boole Press, 1983, pp. 8-16.

3. MacBride Report, p. 18.

4. E. Lloyd Sommerlad, "A New World Communication Order," in Fisher and Harms, *Right to Communicate,* p. 134.

5. Quoted in the MacBride Report, p. 149, n. 1.

6. MacBride Report, p. 149.

7. *Catholic Social Teaching and the U.S. Economy,* Washington, D.C., United States Catholic Conference, 1983.

8. MacBride Report, p. 15.

COMMUNICATION
FOR ALL

CHAPTER ONE

Social Communication and Global Problems

Johan Galtung

There are many global problems involved in the call for a new communication order, and I should like to start by locating them on the political map of the world that I prefer to make use of in my analyses.[1] I divide the world into four parts, combining North-South and East-West divisions so that we have the rich capitalist countries in the northwest, often called the First World; the socialist countries in the northeast, often called the Second World; the poor capitalist countries in the southwest, often called (part of) the Third World, comprising South and Central America, the Caribbean, Africa, western Asia, the Arab world, and southern Asia. Then I add to this a Fourth World, in the southeast: the mainly Buddhist-Confucian countries in eastern and southeastern Asia, in a sense headed by Japan, followed by the mini-Japans (South Korea, Taiwan, Hongkong, Singapore), then the other ASEAN countries, the socialist countries in eastern Asia (above all, the Peoples Republic of China), and—as periphery areas in this vast section of the world—Australia, New Zealand, and Oceania.

The world so divided gives rise to six sets of relationships (see Diagram 1) delimiting six global problem areas:

This paper was first presented to the conference of the International Association for Mass Communication Research (IAMCR), Prague, Czechoslovakia, August 1984.

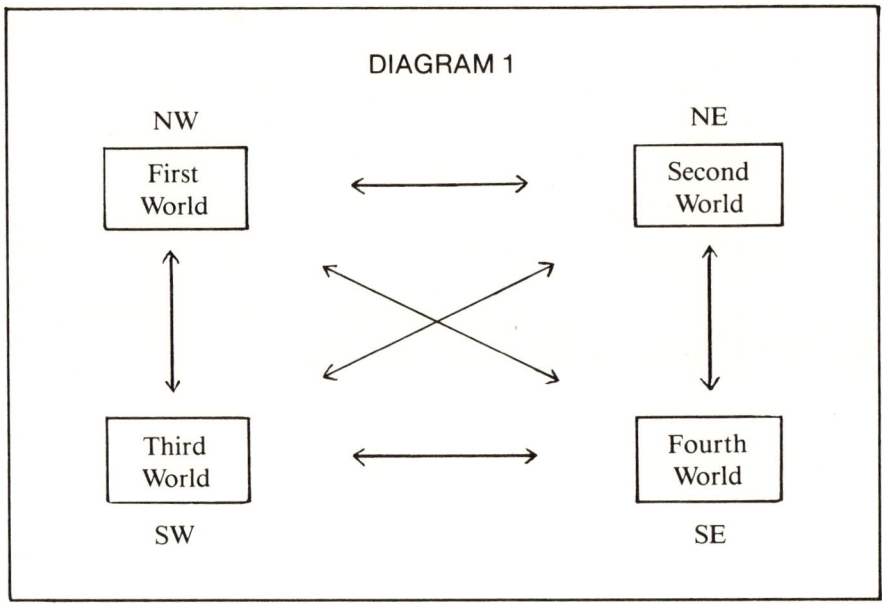

First World-Second World: characterized by a nuclear suicide pact with tremendously serious implications not only for the inhabitants of these two "worlds" but for the rest of humankind as well. The peace/security/disarmament issue is mainly located here.

First World-Third World: characterized by a perennial tendency of the First World to penetrate (sometimes by military intervention) the Third World in order to secure an economic grip on raw materials and inexpensive labor, as well as markets.

First World-Fourth World: characterized by a new phenomenon, although it has been coming for some time: the emergence of Japan and potentially the whole Fourth World as a new player on the world capitalist market. It has shown itself more competent than First World capitalism, beating First World capitalism in general and the U.S.A. in particular at its own game for an increasing range of industrial goods and services.

Second World-Third World: characterized by assistance given in the fight for liberation from colonialism and neocolonialism, with certain efforts to extend control—militarily, politically, and economically—after the struggle is over.

Second World-Fourth World: characterized by, relatively speaking, emptiness; there is little going on. It constitutes a kind of reservation area for world interaction.

Third World-Fourth World: characterized by increasingly heavy penetration of the Third World by the Fourth World, particularly by Japan, making many countries of the Third World look like a Japanese display case. In other words, Japan is not only a success, but a successor to the old colonial powers in the First World.

The problems of over- and under-development are located above all in the First World-Third World relationship, with the First World being increasingly over-developed and the Third World increasingly under-developed, except for tiny elites that have accepted and propagated exogenous models at the expense of endogenous needs. The center/periphery problem is also usually seen as located between the First and the Third World, although it also has Second World-Third World, Second World-Fourth World, and Third World-Fourth World aspects to it.

At any rate, in all these worlds the exploitation of nature is going on, depleting resources and polluting the environment. And the exploitation of human beings is also going on, subordinating human beings to machines, taking away from human beings any sense of mastery of problems they might have had, exhausting and frustrating them, even if they are materially well-off. All of this, of course, is particularly serious with respect to minorities and women, the very young and the very old, and most particularly young and old minority women, all over the world.

In short, ours is a desperately problem-ridden world, full of promises, but also of probabilities that it will get worse.

THE NATURE OF SOCIAL COMMUNICATION

We all know perfectly well that we cannot have all this presented to our minds every day; a selection of events has to be made. There have to be gatekeepers, regulating the flow of information. When I worked on this problem in 1961, I used two simple factors to try to explain why information is communicated the way it is.[2]

The first factor has to do with the center-periphery configuration of the world. There are center countries, located in the First, Second, and now increasingly the Fourth World; and there are periphery countries, mainly in the Third World. This allows for three types of communication relationships, with top priority given to center-center relationships; then come center-periphery relationships (i.e., between a periphery country and its center country); lowest priority is given to periphery-periphery relationships.

These preferences, however, are subject to a variable. On domestic issues, a periphery country, for example, will prioritize center-periphery news. On international issues, it will prioritize center-center news. In either case, periphery-periphery relationships come last, once again.

The second factor has to do with the content of what is being reported, the criteria that events have to satisfy in order to be judged newsworthy. Twelve criteria have been identified. The four most important ones in the present context are the following:

- The more an event concerns elite nations, the more probable that it will become a news item.

- The more an event concerns an elite people, the more probable that it will become a news item.
- The more an event can be seen in personal terms, as due to the action of specific individuals, the more probable that it will become a news item.
- The more negative an event is in its consequences, the more probable that it will become a news item.

As they stand, they look relatively plausible but also somewhat trivial. Writing about this in 1961, I could conclude that the perfect news item would be that Khruschev and Kennedy kill each other during the Vienna summit meeting: top/elite nations; top/elite peoples; highly personal relationship of specific individuals; negative event.

However, these points become less trivial when they are combined. The mock example just mentioned is indicative of an important point in news selection: the cumulative nature of criteria. The more criteria an item satisfies, the more probable that it will become a news item. But this also means that if an event is short on one dimension, it can compensate for it by ranking high in some other dimension. Thus, for nonelite or periphery nations to enter the picture, they have to be "represented" by highly elite persons, preferably heads of state, prime ministers, or possibly foreign ministers. And that immediately gives an overelitist image of periphery countries as countries populated only by elite persons and "the masses."

Correspondingly, the media of center countries can publicize structural (as opposed to personal, actor-oriented) factors, whereas what happens in periphery countries will be seen much more in terms of the actions of individuals. Evidently, what has concrete actors behind it is more newsworthy, an "event." The slow or quick workings of structures—processes—are not events but rather "permanents."[3] Nevertheless, a center country is so newsworthy in and by itself that it may be forgiven for producing permanents and not always events.

Most importantly, news on a periphery country has to be even more negative in order to compensate for the periphery nature of the country. As a consequence the common image of periphery countries in center countries is that of places where only negative things happen, and particularly things that are events rather than permanents: tidal waves, earthquakes, hurricanes, or—as examples of actor-oriented happenings—military coups, assassinations, and the like.

By the same token, the positive, even commonplace, doings of elite persons can make newspaper headlines—when they marry or have children, for instance. Nonelite, ordinary persons will not enter the news through such events, but may do so through murder, family suicide, or the like.

If we now combine these two perspectives, the conclusion is inescapable that reporting on periphery countries will not only be scant, quantitatively insignificant, but also highly negative, and even more so for periphery persons in periphery countries. It is mainly for negative reasons that attention is drawn to their problems: drought, famine, starvation. But it is very important to note that such tragedies are taken out of their structural context—a context partly created and perpetuated by forces in the industrialized world in general and the First World in particular. This type of reporting mainly serves to keep persons in center countries convinced of the miserable living conditions in periphery countries, and consequently of how fortunate they are not to be there.

Let us now look at the global problems again to see how this type of information/communication order will have an impact on our general knowledge and perception of these problems.

When it comes to peace/security/disarmament issues, nothing will fit the bill so well as top-level disarmament conferences. Elite persons from elite nations are meeting, they are addressing each other face to face in highly personal ways, and the only problem is whether the outcome will be positive or negative. As we know, it is usually negative, thus making for "perfect" news. It almost takes participation by heads of state to get positive events through information channels.

But is this not auspicious? Does this not mean that such negotiation will get adequate coverage? No; my point is that the underlying structure of news communication will dominate the perspective on disarmament negotiations much more than vice versa. When lesser dignitaries—say, ambassadors— negotiate, the tendency will be to focus on negative outcomes, and whatever little (positive) they might achieve will be underreported.[4] As a result, pressure will build up for summit meetings, and whatever tiny positive achievement might result will be overreported in an uncritical manner. Needless to say, expectations will tend to be disappointed. The game is then thrown back to a lower level, and the news will make the results look even more meagre. Result: a frustrated public not knowing what to expect or even what to demand.

However, I would be one of the last to want disarmament conferences that are "neutral, balanced, and controlled"; under such conditions they are not able to arrive at results.[5] But because disarmament conferences are actor-oriented phenomena, they constitute news—unlike the continual build-up of arms on both sides, belligerent attitudes, enemy images, the piling-up of unresolved conflict material, and so on. Or, to mention a much more important factor from the other side of the political spectrum: the quantitative and qualitative improvement of the peace movement in West and East, in the First and the Second Worlds, being larger, better prepared, more knowledgeable, better able to exercise pressure on political decision-makers. But only demonstrations are reported.

As regards development issues, there will be the same overreporting on conferences, for they have the great advantage of being events, not permanents. They have visible points in time. Even if they are stretched out over months and years, at least the opening and concluding sessions fall between two editions of a newspaper, or two newscasts on radio or television. Development issues are projected onto the conference schedules and calendars of the year. The constant working of the machineries of exploitation, of the structures of imperialism of various kinds, will of course pass unreported. It may be the subject of articles and books, but will not appear on the front page of a newspaper under the headline "exploitation today about the same as yesterday!" It might be a good idea for a newspaper to have some kind of index of violence, or level of exploitation or repression, somewhere on the top of the front page, as a continual reminder of constant or only slowly changing factors. Direct violence attracts journalists because it is an event; structural violence makes for statistics because it is a permanent. But permanents could be reported in statistical form, and those statistics might not be so unimpressive on front pages as "news" editors seem to think.

Leaving that aside, it is clear that news as we know it will be able to reflect only the tip of the iceberg, the crest of the waves, not the more solid and structure/process type of phenomena occurring all the time. And this will be all the more so for periphery persons, particularly in periphery countries. They will lose what little individuality they have and will disappear into "the masses," particularly in the vocabulary of the left wing, which seems to think it progressive to talk about persons as if they were physical entities (where the word 'mass' comes from). There are of course efforts to see faces in the crowd, to pick up one or two victims of structural violence, and present them with names and addresses. In itself praiseworthy, because humanizing, it is usually done at the expense of any kind of insight into the structures that victimize them. Interest in the personal aspect, the story in human terms, overshadows any interest in socio-political analysis. Earthquakes and hunger become personalized, but there is no analysis of which segments of the population live in housing most easily destroyed by an earthquake, or who are most devastated by a drought when normal water supplies are diverted for use in raising cattle for exportation.

The highly dramatic relationship between the First and the Second Worlds tends to penetrate news having to do with all other relationships among the four worlds; they will be seen in "East-West" terms. In other words, it is not only that center-center relationships dominate quantitatively, but also penetrate qualitatively, other news categories, so that the other five relationships are seen in terms of the first one.

In this connection, it is enlightening to consider how the Fourth World, particularly Japan, is reported. The build-up of the Japanese economy had been going on a very long time, but it went unreported or underreported, because it was a process. Then suddenly it was "discovered" when the First World became worried and called for "voluntary restraints." Just as the grotesque underpayment by the First World for oil went undiscovered until prices suddenly escalated, so the high level of Japanese industrial achievement went unnoticed until its prices suddenly were seen as very low—in other words, highly competitive. What comes suddenly takes on the airs of the devious, of a plot, a conspiracy, whereas the truth is that all of this was completely predictable to anyone familiar with the issues involved and the processes underway.

Again, the point is not that the news has to be written by social analysts. The point is that the world image we receive through the patterns of news communication we are exposed to has a built-in bias in not reporting the continuity in "distant" phenomena. They do not appear threatening, and the more so the further removed from us they are. Contributing to this, of course, are the common misunderstandings about Japan. Japan is thought of as "a part of the West," with little understanding of its cultural and structural specificities. Japan, like China, has its own worldview, its own strategies, different from and even at variance with those of the West.[6]

News Communication as a Function of Western Social Cosmology

Let us now take one step deeper into the structure of news communication. My general thesis is that it cannot be detached from its socio-cultural context, that it is a part of Western ideology/structure in general, what on other occasions I refer to as "social cosmology," and more particularly the Western version.

In that social cosmology I have formulated six themes articulated in terms of news communication.

1. Division of Space

There is a general Western inclination to see the world as divided into two parts, center and periphery, of course with the West in the center. This perspective is found not only in the center, however, but also in the periphery influenced by the West: it also sees itself as the periphery, with the West in the center. News communication is an expression of this, making it common for an African or Latin American country to find very little about a neighboring country in the newspaper, and then only as seen through the eyes of the center country—although this situation has been improving in recent decades.[7]

2. Sources of Negativism

There is in the West a tendency to believe in progress, but also in the possibility of a crisis and after the crisis some kind of *Endzustand,* catharsis. This applies only to the center, however. The periphery does not share in the progress, and particularly if it is an obstinate part of the periphery—one that refuses to be incorporated. This partially explains the negative coloring of news communication: the periphery is a place where, by definition, things go badly, hence negative news from the periphery is correct and objective. But how does this relate to the fact that news from the center also tends to be negative?

I would venture the following hypothesis: negative events are overreported in spite of a general faith in progress; precisely because they are negative, they are news! If they had been positive, they would have been uninteresting, just a part of the general move in the direction of something better—perhaps today somewhat less believed in than before, because of the general idea that there is a crisis going on.

In short, negativism can derive from three sources: the periphery as place where life is negative anyhow; crisis as a phase in a life that is negative anyhow; and the noncrisis center where negative events are exceptional and for that reason become news.

3. Fragmentation of Reality and Knowledge

There is a general inclination in the West to knowledge in terms of atomism and deductivism, a tendency to present reality in a fragmented, scattered way, dividing it into small parts that can be understood and "digested" one at a time; and a tendency to try to tie this together with the help of theoretical frameworks. This mind-set is satisfied by news communicated in the day-to-day reporting that gives prominence to "news-atoms": events limited in space and time to there/then and through the communication channel brought to here/now on the printed page or the newscast, usually coupled with one or more actors whose actions and possible motivations are also reported.

This may seem a reflection of the classical Greek unity of space, time, and action. But it implies an all-consuming division of the world into tiny particles, some of which will be overselected and others underselected, and projected onto the news medium with no connecting links whatsoever, whether inductive or deductive. Such linkage is not necessary: the social cosmology is the connecting link. The basic message is in the structure, not in the content.

4. Nature Subordinated

The Western predatory attitude toward nature is reflected in the way that the media make nature into a nonactor, reporting nature only *für mich* and not *an sich*—not in terms of the balances and development potential of nature. The implication is that any other approach would be anthropomorphic; because nature is seen as so different, so far below the human status, reporting is done in such terms. The projection of the problems of nature goes the same way as the projection of the problems of development and disarmament: into a conference room that satisfies the rules of news reporting.

5. Individualism and Competition

The general drift in the West is toward individualism and verticality—in other words, competition: who wins, and who loses. Whenever a social problem of any kind can be presented this way, it has already made considerable progress toward becoming news. Elections are not seen in terms of whether issues, aspirations, hopes, concerns are adequately articulated, but in terms of who wins and who loses. Politics in general tends to be seen the same way: whether political actors get their programs through the system. Even in the field of culture, music is reported when there is a contest; art and literature are reported in terms of "who is our leading artist" or "novelist." Thus both "personism" and negativism are served: the focus is often much more on the loser than on the winner, on the fading has-been rather than on the rising would-be.

6. The New(s) God

There is a perennial Western theme to the effect that humankind is subordinate to the supernatural, the Supreme Being. However, we are living in a secularizing world, so Supreme Being becomes Supreme Value. And this makes one ask: What is the supreme value of news communication? What is the god of news? Probably just the first three letters of the word "news." News should not be olds, it is about as simple as that. With limited space this means a detachment of the recent from the lasting, of the event from the permanent. This can be counteracted by having analytical articles on the front page and news items further back, as is done in some newspapers of very high quality.[8] But generally the newness of the news will serve as the basic guideline, and will distort the world image in the direction of events.

More concretely, if the accent is on violence, the primacy of newness will focus attention on direct violence rather than structural violence. Media readers/viewers will be conditioned to think of the world in terms of direct, not structural violence. In order to become aware of the workings of structural violence—injustice in the form of institutionalized exploitation—a different level of education is necessary.[9]

Some Consequences

We have the news communication that we deserve. It sells on the market, is demanded by Western consumers, because it is in strict conformity with the underlying social cosmology. If so much in Western societies points in the direction of events that can be seen as competitive between persons and countries struggling or elite positions—often with the emphasis on negative aspects of that struggle—then we get news of that type. Readers/listeners/viewers demand what their subconscious commands. News communication belongs to the picture of freedom, created by the production, distribution, and consumption of distortions of the real world of which one is not aware (because the underlying cosmology is exactly that, *underlying,* in the collective *subconscious*). I imagine the same would be true of a man born in a prison, living his entire life there with other prisoners, but not knowing why he or they were there. He would not think of the prison as a prison; it would be his world, the orbit of his freedom.

And there is another consequence. What happens when individuals become aware of the constraints on news communication—in terms of the quantitative over- and under-representation of certain structural categories and relationships, or in terms of qualitative filters that favor certain types of dramatic news, because it is compatible with the underlying social cosmology? When somebody points this out, and tries to turn the mass media in another direction, less immediately recognizable as a member of a larger family of social-cosmology articulations, it is called "interference with freedom," even "censorship."[10]

Of course, this by no means implies that there could not also be censorship at work in either case. Readers/listeners/viewers can be forced to see only that which is compatible with the background filters. And they can also be forced to have to digest that which is less compatible or even incompatible. Certainly, a "high quality" newspaper giving more attention to periphery persons in periphery countries, showing how structures operate day in and day out, might require a higher educational level. But is that an argument against it? Would it not rather be an argument for making that higher educational level more accessible? Is it not myopic to assume that the image of reality compatible with certain prejudices of one's own civilization is necessarily correct, and that all other images can arise only because of a lack of freedom?

My own position is that this is to a large extent a problem of consciousness and education, not so much of the reader/listener/viewer as of the journalist/editor. However, it is mainly a market problem. Is it not to be expected that there is more demand for the cosmology-compatible than for the cosmology-incompatible? Is it strange if the night editor, as the final filter, makes the headlines supercompatible, cuts out the less perfect from a compatibility view (or gives it low visibility)?

Perhaps much of this boils down to one precise problem: Do we need a *new journalism*, not only new communication and editing? Is consciousness of social-cosmological constraints able to transcend one thought-prison without entering another? Maybe the question is more important than the answer; it will stay with us for some time.

TOWARD A NEW INTERNATIONAL INFORMATION/ COMMUNICATION ORDER?

The background against which the current struggle for NWICO can be seen entails structure and process, power and underlying cultures. I shall make use of it in trying to analyze what is now taking place. In doing so I make two basic assumptions. The first is that the new international *economic* order (NIEO), brought on by the OPEC action in 1973 and the UN special session resolutions of 1974/75, can serve as a model for NWICO.[11] The second assumption is that NWICO will deal more with quantitative, rather than qualitative, dimensions of news communication. Awareness of the underlying factors of the "social cosmology" type I have sketched above will be relatively low. New "order," but no new journalism.

Let us, then, have a look at the new international economic order. It is essentially a structural rearrangement, not meant to challenge capitalism as such but to improve the position of the Third World relative to the First World. NIEO is a process entailing five phases (not necessarily in temporal sequence):

a) better terms of trade for the Third World (leading to decreased North-South trade);
b) more Third World control over productive assets (natural resources, capital, labor, technology);
c) more Third World interaction—South-South trade (TCDC, ECDC);
d) more Third World counterpenetration (investment in "rich" countries, etc.);
e) more Third World influence on world economic institutions: the World Bank, the International Monetary Fund, UNCTAD, transnational corporations.

The first phase is relatively conservative. The division of labor is not challenged, but there is an effort to change the terms of trade so that more processed goods can be obtained for the same amount of unprocessed or semiprocessed goods. In the second phase the Third World goes one step further and tries to control productive assets—if necessary, through nationalization. In the third phase there is emphasis on more Third World interaction—South-South trade in the form of technical and economic cooperation between developing countries.

More interesting from a global perspective are the last two phases. They start with Third World counterpenetration in the sense of investment, buying real estate, stocks and so on, and then more significantly Third World influence on economic institutions such as the World Bank, the International Monetary Fund, and ultimately also transnational corporations.

By and large I think the Third World has not even entered the first stage (except with respect to oil from the OPEC countries). The so-called North-South conflict is essentially a "dialogue" about the first phase, with the Third World becoming less optimistic that the First World has any intention of structural change or of using—dialogue for anything but dialogue—in other words, the purpose of each conference is to prepare the agenda for the next conference.

This, however, does not mean that no process of this kind is verifiable. On the contrary, the *program* as here described for NIEO can be seen as a recapitulation of the *history* of Japanese economic penetration. Carefully watching the terms of trade for their early export products, keeping control of productive assets, and interacting with neighbors in eastern Asia, the Japanese are now certainly at the stage where counterpenetration has come very far: Japan is cooperating with First World partners inside transnational corporations (for instance, carmakers) and for a long time has been in a position to claim second place in the World Bank. It could also be added that the analytical category for this quick progress through the stages necessary in order to arrive at the top of the world capitalist system is not Japan so much as the Fourth World. With the world focusing on Third World claims on the First World, the Fourth World simply goes ahead and translates words into actions. The slow/quick process went undetected.

Returning now to the assumption that NIEO can function as a model for NWICO, certain predictions can safely be made:[12]

a) Better news ratios for the Third World—meaning more news about the Third World in the First World, less about the First World in the Third; better terms of exchange with equal processing levels.
b) Third World control over communication assets—meaning control over which events First World newscasters will extract from the Third World and process into news—and control over local media.
c) More news about other Third World countries in all Third World media, less about the First World.
d) More Third World control in the First World of which events should be processed into news, and control over local media (buying papers and television and radio stations).
e) More Third World control over world communication institutions, including UN agencies and international wire agencies.

Imagine for a moment that this process is carried out with its full range of consequences. Would one then get a balanced picture of the world or an exaggerated picture with the world turned upside down, as seen by eyes accustomed to the present world?

There is some evidence in the direction of the latter alternative. Anybody used to reading the Indian press will know how India-centered it is; the Indian press concentrates almost exclusively on India. Of course, India is, if not a continent, at least a subcontinent. Nevertheless, the rest of the world, including the major center countries, appear in very small news items, and usually in a rather unfavorable light. The Malaysian press and the Caribbean press, to take two other examples, concentrate on their own regions. Their former "mother" countries receive much less attention.

In other words, the process in this field is already on the way, and has been on the way for some time. But there is one major instance where the process has even come much further than that for the NIEO. I am thinking of the fifth and final phase, where there is little in terms of Third World control of international wire agencies. There is an effort in Third World countries to set up their own, such as Prensa Latina and the International Press Service (IPS),[13] but this is not the same thing as penetrating and even partly controlling the giants in the field—Reuters (originally designed for stock exchange reports), AP, UPI, AFP, TASS, and so on. The reason for this is that the Third World already commands the forum chosen for this structural transformation: UNESCO. And the result is well known: the Western accusation, led by the United States, that this constitutes one more example of "politicization," and the threatened withdrawal of the United States from UNESCO.[14]

In this one would have to admit that the United States has fully understood the significance of what is going on. In one sense a new international information/communication order would be even more important than a new international economic order. It would make everyone look at the world differently. Third World residents would be much better informed about their own countries and regions, and less mesmerized by foreign powers and superpowers. They would view the world differently, with the First World seen as a dangerous place, exposed to sudden, unexpected events, partly from nature, partly from malicious individuals inside the social structure. They would see their own countries more in continuity with the past, as a structure unfolding in a sometimes slow, sometimes quick, process. Instead of seeing the center as the part of the world from which salvation comes, it will be seen as a place where world-threatening dangers originate, among them the possibility of a nuclear war. In short, they would have a more realistic perception of the contemporaneous world. But also a new thought prism.

One big question, however, is whether this is really going to happen or whether the First World, and to some extent perhaps also the Second World, will understand this and intervene through their various channels. More particularly, I am thinking of First World control of whatever goes into producing a newspaper, for instance. There is newsprint; then the labor needed in the form of trained journalists; the capital needed to finance the enterprise; the research needed not only to get events transformed into news but also to understand the whole process; and finally an administration, which is management of a sometimes very difficult kind. The only answer to such a strategy would be for Third World countries to become independent vis-à-vis all five production factors, singly or together with other countries in the same situation.[15] It would be best for this to be done in a pluralistic manner with different types of news media within any given Third World country and with several new wire agencies coexisting, each one with its own particular speciality or tendency, rather than one recipe common to them all. We have had more than enough of one recipe in the world, with the Western tradition that points to itself as a paragon of freedom, in spite of all the constraints under which it operates.

But let us speculate a little further. Let us assume that the successful part of the world right now, economically speaking, is not the First World with its cries, nor the Second World with its rigidity bordering on stagnation, nor the Third World with its bottomless misery and increasing discrepancy between elites and the general population, but the Fourth World, where to a large extent both elites and the general population seem to be undergoing processes of economic growth in a fairly parallel manner. If this is the case, how would it be reflected in a new international information/communication order?

It is difficult to tell. I think any analysis of the structure of foreign news since the mid-1960s would reveal very clearly how much more prominent the Fourth World has become in First World news reporting. It has probably also become much more prominent in its own news reporting.[16] But what about the Third World? Has the Third World really discovered what goes on in eastern Asia or is it still basically obsessed by First World-Third World relationships, with an occasional element of Second World events, to the exclusion of the rather major part of the world in eastern and southeastern Asia? Does the Third World still tend to see Japan as a part of the West, which it evidently is not, and the other countries as a part of the South, which they also evidently are not, as witnessed by their very rapid industrialization and increasing share in the world market?

I mention this because it should be remembered that the West is not the only civilization in the world that sees itself as the center. So does China, perceiving the rest less as periphery than as *barbarian,* dangerous, exotic, but definitely not something of which China is a part. And does not Japan also see itself as a center, with a tendency to see the rest of the world as one big *resource,* in earlier stages for market and advanced technology, in later stages for market and raw materials?[17] Would that, then, not lead to a news image with other parts of the world becoming exotic, but distant, dangerous places that exist *für mich* and not *an sich*? And, if this is coupled with a possible major revolution where telematics is concerned, giving a certain ascendency to Japan with teleprinters, telex, and the like, would the conclusion not be that the new international information/communication order could be like the old one, only with the center in the Fourth World rather than in the First?

I doubt it for one simple reason: the centers in the Fourth World do not have the same missionary interest in propagating themselves, their values and structures, as does the First World. Propagation of products certainly, yes, out of commercial interest—but that is something else. It is more likely that Fourth World countries will have a relatively self-contained news system, circulating detailed news among themselves, being less interested in what goes on in *Barbaria* and *Resourcia,* except insofar as it is directly relevant to their own undertakings.

So the statistical distribution of news items will probably become less First World centered. But neither the Second nor the Third World will command enough economic/political/cultural power to say: we are the new centers (or, more precisely, they may *say* so, but not convince many, perhaps not even themselves). The Fourth World has the *economic power*, also considerable political and cultural *Ausstrahlung*. But its worldview is different; it may be less interested in being seen as *the* center.

Hence, the situation is perhaps not so bad. A center is slowly being dethroned, and there is no obvious successor. A more symmetric world image is possible. What a challenge for a truly global newspaper, and not only one, many! And not like the *International Herald Tribune,* so extremely biased toward the West generally and the United States, its country of origin, in particular. We need other efforts, more efforts. We not only need a *new* journalism, but a *global* journalism, problem-conscious, socially conscious, at home in the world as a whole.

CONCLUSION: TOWARD A NEW AND GLOBAL JOURNALISM

In this effort to look for some major lines in the structure and process of international news information and communication, there are two phenomena that warrant closer examination.

First, I do not think there is any doubt that a quantitative transformation is going on, with somewhat less emphasis on the center, and somewhat more emphasis on the periphery. However, I am not at all sure that this is accompanied by a similar qualitative transformation where the character of what is regarded as news is changed. With more power to the periphery, both on the printed page and in the production of news, it is not at all clear that the product has changed. It might, in fact, even have become worse, as it also has in many newspapers and in much radio and television reporting in the First World, with even more elitism, personism, and negativism than ever before. The front page of a newspaper degrades itself, its journalists, its readers, and all those concerned, when it presents rape and murder as the major constituents of world society. And this is sometimes called "the personal touch!"

Secondly, social communication has hardly become much more relevant to global problems than before, and may even have become increasingly counter productive. The vast array of detached space/time events presented as news are seen as a set of events, not a set of problems. A problem has a beginning in its roots and a possible end in its solution; along the way *alternatives* have to blossom, as also carriers of those alternatives and *strategic actors* have to be mobilized or at least pointed to. But this is not the way reporting is generally done. All such factors are regarded commonly to be "ideological," "biased," not worthy of attention, using up too much valuable news space.

In short: I do not think much progress is being made. The structure is sliding and jumping over the globe—but remains basically the same. The content is about the same, relevant but biased. A new order is not enough. We need a new journalism, and a global journalism, liberated from visible and invisible repression, capable of reflecting in its social communication the global nature of our problems.

NOTES

1. See my article, "On the Dialectic between Crisis and Crisis Perception," *International Journal of Comparative Sociology,* 1984, 1–2, pp. 4–32.

2. See Johan Galtung and Mari Holmboe Ruge, "The Structure of Foreign News: The Presentation of the Congo, Cuba and Cyprus Crisis in Four Norwegian Newspapers," chap. 4, in *Essay in Peace Research,* Copenhagen, Ejlers, 1980. (Originally published in *Journal of Peace Research,* 1965, no. 1.)

3. For further elaboration of this distinction from a methodological point of view, see my *Methodology and Ideology,* Copenhagen, Ejlers, 1977, esp. chaps. 8 and 9.

4. Thus, because negative outcomes are seen as normal, negative news passes through the filter, and is compatible with the anonymity of lower-level functionaries. When higher-level personages are involved, positive news may more easily be permitted, even should appear. Consider the (in my view) overoptimistic reporting on the meeting between the two superpower foreign ministers, Schultz and Gromyko, in Geneva in January 1985.

5. Nine reasons why disarmament negotiations tend to fail are given in chap. 4 of my *There Are Alternatives: Four Roads to Peace and Security,* Nottingham, Spokesman Books, 1984.

6. See, for instance "The Chinese Path to Development," *Review,* 1982, pp. 460-86,

and "On the Possible Decline and Fall of Japan," *East Asia,* Berlin, Campus, vol. I, 1983.

7. I am thinking particularly of the tendency of developing countries to report what happens in other developing countries.

8. *El Pais* and *Le Monde,* for example.

9. See the excellent research done by Helga Theunert and Bernd Schorb, *Gewalt in Fernsehen und ihre sozialen Folgen,* Munich, Institut Jugend-Film-Fernsehen, February 1983.

10. I am, of course, thinking of the UNESCO debate in connection with the very important report by the MacBride commission, *Many Voices, One World,* UNESCO 1980 (the title is beautiful, but given the way the press has been standardized by Western styles, the title, "One Voice, Many Worlds," might have been more appropriate).

11. For a view of NIEO as a process, see "The New International Economic Order and the Basic Needs Approach," *Alternatives,* 1978-79, pp. 455-76.

12. See also the article "Towards a New International Technological Order," *Alternatives,* 1978-79, pp. 277-300.

13. In due time the creation of the IPS will stand out as a divide in the entire history of international and news reporting, and the audacious and important work of Roberto Savio, Marc Nerfin, and others in that connection will be duly appreciated.

14. That withdrawal became effective January 1, 1985, an event that in my view should be welcomed as an opportunity for UNESCO to work on these important matters without the procrastination characteristic of one former member state. UNESCO, for its part, should contemplate slashing staff salaries by 25 percent—corresponding to the US contribution. Those salaries are much too high, and easily attract money-oriented rather than task-oriented personnel.

15. Again, IPS stands out as a concrete effort in that direction.

16. Thus, the boisterous, quite self-conscious Japanese reporting on Japan is today rather different from what it was only 15 years ago.

17. See my "Japan and Future World Politics," in *Essays in Peace Research,* Vol. 5, pp. 169-205.

CHAPTER TWO

Strengths and Weaknesses of the New International Information Empire

Herbert I. Schiller

It was in 1973 that the leaders of the Non-Aligned Movement met in Algiers and charged that the international information system promoted cultural domination and contributed to the general state of dependency of Latin America, Asia, and Africa.[1]

There have been many meetings since. Evidence confirming the accuracy of the early accusations has accumulated. An International Commission for the Study of Communication Problems issued one hundred monographs as well as a comprehensive report, *Many Voices, One World* (UNESCO, 1980). New international bodies have been created to deal with some of the problems emphasized in the studies.

This is an appropriate time to survey the international informational scene and determine where matters now stand. What is the current state, for example of the production and sale of cultural goods and services in the world market? Has it changed significantly since 1973? Are there new developments—the new information technologies, for instance—that change the parameters of the entire debate? In any case, under whose auspices are the new electronic technologies, computers and satellites especially, being installed and used in

---

This paper was first prepared for the conference "Theology and the Communications Media," Trinity Conference Center, West Cornwall, Connecticut, June 6-10, 1983.

the international economy? Do these developments lessen or intensify domination-dependency relationships between nations? Finally, what are the political and legal forms that the emergent international information order requires and attempts to create?

Answers to these questions can here only be partial and limited. What follows may provide some sense of the present and future drift of the global cultural/informational condition.

THE CURRENT GLOBAL STATE OF PRODUCTION AND SALE OF CULTURAL GOODS AND SERVICES

In recent years there has been at least partial recognition of the flood of media material that moves largely in one direction, mostly though not entirely from the United States to the rest of the world. In 1974 a study documented one aspect of this condition, describing the world flow of television programming in an apt title, "Television Traffic—A One-Way Street."[2]

What the authors of that report called attention to was not a passing phenomenon, taking place only at the beginning of the television age. Since then, other studies have given accounts of U.S. and Western media penetration in Latin American, Asian, and African countries. These studies confirm and specify the massive presence *in 1984*, of Western, mostly American, material on movie and television screens and in the newspapers, magazines, and books of most nations.

Ignoring or denying this condition for years, some Western media are now compelled, by the evidence and the outcry, to acknowledge, however grudgingly, that the complaints have some justification. The *International Herald Tribune*, a U.S.-owned newspaper published in Paris, quoted the following in an editorial:

> *Dallas* and other [television] series already amortized economically by their sales in the United States are offered to world television at rates which tend to undermine local programming. . . . It is not a trivial point in countries with underdeveloped local television, meager local resources, and little alternative diversion.[3]

True enough, but the *Tribune* errs in regarding this as something affecting only the less economically developed countries. In Italy, for example, it was reported at the end of 1982 that national television channels not only are filled with American programming, but that the largest Italian chains have made arrangements with the three major U.S. networks to import their outputs almost in their entirety.[4]

And in the Philippines:

> TV networks, broadcasting 573.5 hours weekly (almost entirely "entertainment"), include 58 percent foreign canned prime-time American

series like "Charlies' Angels" and "S.W.A.T.," and a few Japanese robot cartoon programs. Even the government "Voice of the Philippines," charged with broadcasting the nation's culture overseas, runs a sign-on to sign-off canned radio format of American "easy listening" music imported from the Kala Music Company in Kalamazoo, Michigan [Sussman, "Telecommunication," p. 51].[5]

An article in *Le Monde Dimanche* reports the fascination of Algerians for the U.S. television serial "Dallas."[6] *Advertising Age* believes that Peru "may be emerging from the dark ages" because television and newspapers have been returned to private ownership and "among the 10 top-rated programs in Peru, seven are U.S. imports, including 'Starsky and Hutch,' the No. 1 program of Peruvian TV." In addition, a new TV channel, beginning operation in November 1982, will broadcast "99 percent imported programs."[7]

These are the conditions, much the same in most parts of the globe, that provide the background for the appeal of the former French minister of culture, Jack Lang, before a UNESCO-organized meeting in Mexico City in July 1982, for a "real cultural resistance, a veritable crusade against—let us call things by their true name—the financial and intellectual imperialism that rarely appropriates territories, but appropriates consciousness. It appropriates ways of thinking and ways of living."[8]

Lang, who spoke before an overwhelmingly supportive audience, largely drawn from Third World nations, was bitterly criticized by many intellectuals in France, and the U.S. media in general, for these remarks.

Lang replied that he was not attacking individual artists and that it is essential to distinguish between creative individuals and the multinational firms that now run the international informational-cultural industries.[9] This distinction is critical and must be insisted upon because the transnational media prefer to blur this point, or overlook it entirely.

Another sanguine view is that the situation is a temporary one, and that sooner or later all nations will develop their own cultural capabilities, television programming in particular. Developments in Mexico, Brazil, and a few other countries are believed to support this optimism. Yet these examples do nothing to contradict the essential conditions of transnational corporate domination of global cultural informational production. Those few national media systems with programming capability repeat, with rare exceptions, the formulas of the dominant centers. More importantly, they are heavily financed by the same transnational companies that fill their circuits with product-marketing commercials.

The hard fact remains that transnational corporations (TNCs) today are the dominant elements in the international economic order. And national media systems increasingly are being enlisted to provide the infrastructure for disseminating TNC economic and ideological philosophy. Symptomatic of this condition, the chief advertisers, who supply financial support to the media, especially television and the press, are generally the giant companies, mostly in the consumer products field. The Philippine situation is in no way atypical:

> Of the 123 members of the Philippine Association of National Advertisers, 75 percent are TNCs or their affiliates, and on one national TV channel in that country, nine of the ten largest sponsors are TNCs such as Pepsi Cola, Colgate, and Nestle [Sussman, "Telecommunications"].

What this pattern appearing in scores of countries demonstrates, is that the penetration and often saturation of national communications systems with U.S. and Western programming and advertising is not some peripheral cultural problem, affecting a vague, imprecise entity called "national identity." It is, in fact, the daily and continuous construction of an economic order and value system in which the acquisition of consumer goods and services, to the near total disregard of the needs of the social and public sphere, is repeatedly emphasized with the most skilled communication techniques ever devised. It is, in fact, an essential part of the process by which individuals and nations are assimilated to a market-organized development model.

Drawing on the centuries-old British experience, Jeremy Seabrook explains what is at the end of this developmental road. He compares what has happened to the peoples of the U.K. who have "enjoyed" this development model for over two hundred years, with what has been done to the colonized peoples of Africa and Asia:

> We have been victims of the same fraud that we have seen in the desperate dependent economies of the Third World. This is what all the shrillness and stridency of selling has meant, a deepening subordination of people to market relationships instead of human ones. . . . For a long time we were unable to recognize the nature of this violent disturbance of our lives, for reasons that are obvious. It provided us release from an earlier, scarcely bearable, poverty . . . but instead, capital . . . has known, not only to take from us our labour, our sweat and muscle, but how to insinuate itself into the heart and mind and imagination.[10]

This is a new kind of despoliation that is now being visited upon the already ravished ex-colonial world—the capture of minds. In the wake of exploited labor and plundered natural resources, there is now the massive effort of corporate-financed media (and other consciousness-shaping forces as well) to pull entire peoples into the consumerist trap.

NEW INFORMATION TECHNOLOGIES AND NWICO

While the expanding transnational corporate order continues to avail itself of—actually, to overwhelm—national media, a new and still more potent means has appeared in recent years to facilitate and extend still further the power of the great transnational companies. The rapid development and improvement of new electronic information technologies has offered an enormously enhanced range of operations to transnational business and its military protective shield.

The new technologies were originally developed and installed to expedite and administer the worldwide deployment of U.S. military power. Now, powerful computer networks, linked by communication satellites, constitute a global infrastructure for corporate business as well as military oversight around the world.

The volume of data now moving invisibly across national boundaries—called transborder data flows—remains unknown, because the businesses concerned do not care to reveal the scope of their activities. In fact, they take precautions to prevent that kind of information from becoming public.[11] In any case, what is happening quietly, almost unremarked in public and political life, is the reorganization of the world by giant private structures, utilizing new electronic communication technologies. In this transformational process, information plays a vital part in productive, distributive, administrative, and general education-cultural functionings.

It is, in consequence, entirely insufficient to view cultural control, at this point, as largely a matter of media domination and message/image-flow imbalance. It includes this, to be sure, but *of great and growing importance is the remodeling of the entire information system that is being effected by a few market economies*—those of the United States and Japan in particular, but also those of France, the U.K., and West Germany.

In this remodeling, information occupies the primary position because now it can be used decisively in industrial processes—informatized productive systems—as well as in its customary use in administrative and educational spheres. However, the manner in which information is being generated, processed, transmitted, stored, retrieved, and disseminated is the key to understanding the sweeping institutional changes now occurring nationally and internationally.

It is perhaps obvious, but it is still important to point out that the new information technologies were developed *in, by,* and *for* highly advanced capitalist economies—that of the U.S.A. in particular. It is to be expected therefore, that these technologies are now being employed single-mindedly to serve market objectives. Control of the labor force, higher productivity, capture of world markets, and continued capital accumulation are the propelling influences under which the new information technologies are deployed.

An added feature, derivative of the great capabilites of the new instrumentation, is the extension of the market into several fields and activities that had been regarded as unprofitable but now can be put on a profit-making basis. This is especially observable in areas that have historically constituted the public sector. In health, hospital care, public administration, education, and public services in general, private initiatives undergirded with the new technologies are replacing or eliminating traditional public responsibility and accountability.

What the growing practice of making information a commodity is doing to the information-cultural condition in the already industrialized nations—and here again the United States is in the forefront of this development—is a subject well worth serious study. Here it can only be said that an ever widening gap, between those with and those without access to information, is more and more evident. The long-term consequences of a society divided into information "haves" and "have nots" have barely begun to be acknowledged, much less acted upon.[12]

In the poorer parts of the world where almost three-quarters of the world population lives, the appearance of global information systems, directed by and of advantage to the power centers of a few nation-states, threatens to create a new, worldwide system of domination/dependency, exceeding anything that has existed up to this time. Anthony Smith writes:

> The threat to independence in the late twentieth century from the new electronics could be greater than was colonialism itself. . . . For many societies [communications satellites] may become the pipettes through which the data which confers sovereignty upon a society is extracted for processing in some remote place.[13]

Poor nations and their leaders, nonetheless if they are not voluntarily seeking it out, are being cajoled into the new technologies "race" with glowing promises that electronics instrumentation offers the means of moving speedily out of "backwardness" into the twenty-first century. The public relations campaigns are powerful and effective. Besides, the technical capabilities of the new technologies are fascinating and often compelling.

But, as with technology in general, it is the social matrix within which it is developed and employed that ultimately determines the benefits it produces or denies, as well as who are to be beneficiaries and victims. At present, the matrix is a transnational corporate structure, reinforced by a globally interventionist military machine. These are the users who find the new technologies enormously helpful and benefit-producing.

A study of the international banking sector, for example, demonstrates convincingly that the new instrumentation presents the transnational banks with a great opportunity "to escape governmental control on the international flow of capital."[14] A senior associate with the Carnegie Endowment for International Peace, discussing international transactions of the most powerful U.S. transnational bank, has said:

> The overriding issue . . . is the ability of banks like Citibank to deliberately subvert the rules and policies of sovereign governments. While banks and funds move freely across national borders, bank regulators and government authorities do not.[15]

There are many other advantages for the TNCs, some operational, others political and ideological. They can be realized in industrially developed as well as in less industrialized nations. The sanctions, for example, that the Reagan administration imposed on European nations continuing to honor their contracts for supplying equipment for the Euro-Siberian gas pipeline revealed how the control of information, in a computerized transnational system, can operate. When the U.S. government acted against the French affiliate of an American-based TNC—an affiliate that had continued to ship parts to the U.S.S.R. under its contract—the government merely instructed the parent firm in the U.S.A. to turn off the information supply to its affiliate. *Business Week* reported:

> All Dresser [Dresser Industries, Inc.] had to do to comply with Reagan's embargo was to change the entry key to a computer in Pittsburgh on August 26 [1982], the day the sanctions took effect. That effectively barred Dresser's French subsidiary from access to the technology it needs to complete orders it has on the books and to compete for new ones. . . . Without access to Dresser's computerized data bank, Dresser-France's engineers lack vital information to build the made-to-order compressors that account for about three-quarters of the company's business.[16]

It is not by chance that critical information is stored in the home country, the United States. It is also noteworthy that the victimized firm in this instance was located in France, hardly a Third World nation.

If this can happen to a "core" West European country, then whose interests may the informational systems and connections now being installed in Third World countries be expected to serve? Will poor countries, as they are being led to believe, find opportunities in the new instrumentation to create their own, autonomous developmental course, widen their health and educational systems, and, overall, enrich the lives of their peoples?

The evidence, at this stage, certainly is not conclusive. Yet there are warning signals flashing in numerous locales! A member of the Zairian Permanent Consultative Committee on Informatics describes how useful, actually indispensable, the new technologies are for foreign mining companies, banks, and ore-shipping firms that extract Zairian natural resources and ship them abroad. Bukassa Bukassa writes:

> These MNFs [multinational firms] have subsidiaries implemented on the sites with representatives in the capital city. These representative offices need to be linked with headquarters in Europe, the U.S.A., or Japan as well as with factories in other parts of Zaire. . . . Telematics in Zaire appears to be the child of MNFs and their banks. . . . It was someone abroad who, needing the connections, suggested implementing them in Zaire. The implemented network operates according to the already existing pattern of circulation of goods. How can such a network induce

new prospects of progress and development for the country in which it is operating?[17]

Consider the following announcement of a Caribbean Basin Telecommunications Conference held in May 1983 in Jamaica:

> Caribbean/Central American Action (CCAA), a . . . non-profit, Washington-based organization funded by about 60 major U.S. businesses, is assisting the Caribbean Basin countries meet their economic development goals through linkages with the U.S. business community. To help strengthen Caribbean Basin business organizations and encourage U.S. investment and trade within the region, CCAA is launching its own Caribbean Information Network and data base in cooperation with Control Data Corporation with affiliates in the Caribbean, Central America, Canada, and Great Britain. . . .
>
> This conference is vitally important to the Carribean Basin countries—in helping them leapfrog over time and take full advantage of the new technologies in greatly enhancing and facilitating information flow—and to U.S. companies—by giving them a distinct edge in helping Caribbean countries meet those needs.
>
> The Conference will be sponsored by a group of companies representing telecommunications, information technologies and services, and television programming. Sponsors confirmed are: GTE, AT&T International, ITT Dialcom, IBM, Northern Telecom, Control Data, and Comsat.[18]

Are the arrangements that draw patently vulnerable and weak economies into electronic communication networks exceptional? Are there more flexible linkages, potentially beneficial to the user society, whatever its place in the global division of labor? Again, the last word has not been spoken.

Such prospects will depend heavily on the economic strength of the receiver society, the level of popular awareness and mobilization, and the degree to which leadership in these societies insists on autonomy and independence. It will also depend heavily on the degree of involvement in the international market economy and, in particular, the connection with the transnational forces in that economy.

How these separate factors interact in a national context makes prediction about the consequences of satellite-computer connections for a specific state uncertain at best. The case of Brazil is illustrative. Vast in territory, rich in resources, well along in industrial development, Brazil also is heavily in debt to transnational banks and suffers greatly with fluctuations in raw material prices that often cut deeply into its export revenues. Intent on following a national path to development yet choosing the Western developmental model, Brazil is enmeshed in the transnational system despite its efforts to encourage national property interests. In information policy, for example, it has tried valiantly to create a domestic information sector that permits national decision-making in this vital area.

The results thus far, though not conclusive, have been less than satisfactory. An official governmental report describes in general terms the character of the problems encountered:

> Transborder data flow links are not only used to move data internationally, but also to shift such information resources as managerial and engineering skills, computer power, technology developments, data-base management systems, specialized software, and intelligence in general. Given the prevailing global distribution and administration of information and skills, transborder data flows tend to facilitate their concentration in developed countries. . . . If projected linearly, this could lead, in the long run, to an intellectual impoverishment of the societies of developing countries ["Brazil"].[19]

Substantiating this analysis, the users of the Brazilian nationally administered high technology system are almost entirely transnational corporations. Twenty-seven of its twenty-nine international communication links fall into this category. "The non-Brazilian transnational corporations are all among the world's largest 100 corporations, headquartered mostly in the United States." Most significantly of all, "most information resources are located in the United States, irrespective of the type of user and the type of data flow" (ibid.).

The satellite networks linking computers and data bases around the world have not yet totally recast the international division of labor into a sharply divided array of information suppliers and information processors, the latter exercising the commanding roles. Yet the major users of the new systems work toward these ends. International or not, market dynamics make it almost inevitable that the present producers and users of sophisticated information technology will try to restructure world production, trade, and culture to their own interests and needs. These interests, in brief, are unimpeded profit-seeking and maintenance of the prevailing relationships between nations and classes. The control of information has now become a primary means to achieving these ends.

TNC INTERESTS IN THE INTERNATIONAL POLITICO-LEGAL ARENA

Beyond the daily economic routines that establish the de facto configurations of domination and dependency, special initiatives are also required to enable the overall process to move ahead. Considerable and intensifying efforts—political, legal, psychological, and economic—are being expended by U.S.-based transnational interests to overcome resistance and smooth the way for what is hoped will be a polished, modernized, and long-lasting world "leadership" position. That these efforts must be made, however, indicates also that there are numerous obstacles still in the way. Not least of these is a near global demand for human equality and the economic betterment of disadvantaged peoples. Hence the reluctance of Third World nations to accept dependency and subordination.

These sentiments vary in intensity from place to place, and the means to realize them are generally weak and uneven. They find strong support in large, international, humanitarian organizations, some of which have been established since the end of World War II. Others date back to the beginning of the twentieth century.

In these fora, a struggle proceeds, invariably pitting the weaker, poorer nations against the few stronger, more economically powerful ones, though, on any specific issue, shifting positions and coalitions may emerge. Divisions have been evident since at least the mid-1960s. They coincide generally with the expansion of the international system to include the more than one hundred new nations that have come into existence after the breakup of the old European empire systems.

Although with some oversimplification, the disputes may be said to cluster around the efforts of the large majority of (poorer) nations to change the economic, political, and cultural rules that govern the conditions of life and the division of wealth and authority globally. In this contest, the United States, defending the powerful transnational interests that predominate domestically and internationally, stand with a few supporters, mostly West European states, Japan, and a handful of additional allies, against the overwhelming majority of nations and of the world population.

The short-term goal of the transnational groupings, under American leadership, is to use the new information technologies to shape a global system that, in effect, will allow the continued political, cultural, and economic domination of most of the planet under new forms and orderings. Though this objective is beyond accomplishment in any realistic long-term perspective, great energies currently are being expended, especially in the decisive informational-communications sphere, where the transnational corporate system is, at the same time, most powerful and most vulnerable.

Strength comes from the great flexibility and control that the new information technologies provide to the worldwide business system. Vulnerability, however, accompanies this strength because there is also an enormous dependency of the system on unrestricted, open circuits for the flood of messages the system initiates and transmits. Vulnerability also resides in the necessity for *national* agreements for the transmission of messages as well as on the physical location of communication facilities—that is, the stationing of satellites in specific spatial orbits, for example.

For these reasons, international negotiations over information and communication issues touch the exposed nerves of the transnational corporate order. To be sure, this is hardly the picture that comes across to the average media consumer in the West. In most American reporting, for example—and there are notable, though few exceptions—it appears that forces of tyranny are waging relentless war on freedom of expression. What this presentation overlooks or conceals is that the central issue at stake is the control of the world system of information, either for the privileged use of concentrated private power—which is what the "free-flow" now sustains—or for new possibilities that can scarcely be identified at this time, but that represent the hope of many for nonexploitive economic and cultural modes of existence.

Accordingly, it is understandable, if lamentable, that the great bulk of Western news and informational sources are something less than forthright when touching on these crucial systemic matters, many of which could affect the character of their own future activities.

It is also clear why the basic U.S. policy in international communications remains, as it has since the 1940s, an unequivocal demand for a "free flow of information." The vigor with which this position is expressed has increased in proportion to the increased dependency of the transnational business system on international data transmissions and information flow. Now the "free-flow chorus," along with governmental representatives, includes bank executives, airline and data-processing company presidents and, as vociferous as ever, the leaders of the big communications conglomerates.

However, the allure of the free-flow position has diminished greatly since the early days of the United Nations and UNESCO, in the 1950s, when the U.S. view went almost unopposed. Now, though still maintained with great stridency by its supporters, it encounters stiff and mounting opposition in one international forum after another.

In reaction to this opposition, there is a hardening effort, not yet totally subscribed to by all segments of influential American decision-making, that seeks to deny the legitimacy of long-established international bodies concerned with information and communication matters, and to press for undemocratic changes in their structures. At the conclusion of the World Administrative Radio Conference, in 1979, for example, the United States government reevaluated its relationship to the International Telecommunications Union (ITU), the organization with responsibility for the allocation and management of the international radio frequency spectrum and the geostationary orbit for communication satellites. An official study, prepared by the Office of Technology Assessment for the U.S. Senate Committee on Commerce, Science, and Transportation, came to these conclusions:

The world has changed. There are scores of new, independent, poor nations, participating in international regulatory and administrative organizations. They seek to change the existing allocation of benefits and privileges, which are lopsidedly in favor of a few industrialized states and the most powerful users in those countries. The United States is not only unwilling to make these concessions but, in fact, seeks to obtain a greater share of scarce global resources to meet the needs of its transnational enterprises and its global military force. And, finally, in international gatherings where these issues are discussed, and (at least in the past) decided upon, the likelihood that U.S. interests will get their way grows more doubtful.[20]

What to do? A U.S. government assessment panel outlined a few options:

—Abandon the ITU altogether "and establish a more congenial grouping of developed countries as a forum for coordination to avoid radio interference, and simply ignore other countries."
—Abandon the "one-nation, one-vote" formula, and change the voting system to "one more fair to the United States, perhaps giving added voting weight to those countries that contribute most heavily to the United Nations budget."
—"Force a revision of the "one-nation, one-vote" formula to one that would reflect the dominance of these nations in the actual use of the spectrum."[21]

In sum, the recommendations proposed by the assessment panel, for U.S. adoption in the ITU, advocate antidemocratic voting procedures and, failing their adoption, the abandonment of international agreement in favor of unilateral decisions based on economic and technological strength.

Similar strategies are being pursued in other international organizations such as the United Nations and UNESCO. In the case of the latter body, the president of the United States has threatened to withdraw the American financial contribution to it if it refuses to follow the "free-flow of information" policies enunciated by the United States.[22]

Despite these intimidating moves, and against strong U.S. opposition, the United Nations General Assembly, in December 1982, approved a declaration of "principles governing the use by States of artificial earth satellites for international direct television broadcasting." One hundred eight nations endorsed the right of nations to *prior consent* over incoming, direct-broadcast, satellite messages. This was essentially a reassertion of the sovereign rights of states, faced with a powerful new technology of great penetrative strength, to order their national cultural-informational space in accordance with their own desires and with respect for international law. But, as has been the case consistently when international information questions have been at issue, Western (especially U.S.) media have referred to sentiments and actions for national autonomy as threatening, undemocratic, and restrictive.[23]

The penchant of U.S. policymakers to identify corporate message traffic as a "free flow of information" is hardly new. Yet the inclination to regard domestic legal arrangements supportive of these interpretations as inviolable international codes grows more audacious. In fact, the effort to have U.S. law take precedence over legal authority elsewhere has become a steadily growing phenomenon.

A recent Royal Institute of International Affairs study on "the problem of extraterritoriality" found that the United States has adopted an "assertive" extraterritorial jurisdiction, which has increased since the 1940s and "the trend has clearly been upward." This stance runs parallel with what is termed "increasing interdependence" among states, but which actually describes the great growth of transnational influence internationally. "Since World War II, multinational corporations with two or more affiliates established under the jurisdiction of different nations have become the most significant enterprises engaged in international commerce" (Rosenthal and Knighton, *National Laws*, p. 1).[24]

Extraterritoriality has to do with "the general problem of conflicting claims by nation-states to apply their laws and implement their policies to affect conduct outside their territory in a way which may undermine and conflict with the laws and policies of a foreign government" (ibid., p. viii).

Extraterritoriality is no new feature of international relations. A new context now prevails but the claims are familiar. The U.S. "aggressive approach to extraterritorial enforcement" (ibid., p. 8), is a function of the power of the American transnational system. It arises because "the wealthier and more powerful you are, the more difficult it is for others to resist your actions." Accordingly, "U.S. extraterritoriality increased as the United States became an international power, and as European nations were especially dependent upon the United States for economic assistance—during the 1940s and early 1950s" (ibid., p. 9).

Yet the ability to maintain and extend U.S. information and communication domination by resorting to the extraterritorial invocation of U.S. law—insisting on the international applicability and desirability of the First Amendment in the U.S. Constitution, as interpreted by transnational corporations, for example—is no long-term guarantee for maintaining present privileges in the international economic and informational order. For law, no less than communication, can become a two-way street: "Those countries which see themselves as victims of extraterritoriality are becoming more vigorous in their responses" (ibid., p. 31). This too, is not entirely a new or nonrecurrent phenomenon in world history.

But how the reactions of the "victims" are, and will be, presented to the American public via the U.S. media is another matter entirely. It is distressing but true that information control will have, and does have, a profound effect on the ability of the transnational corporate system to retain the allegiance, or at least not to incur the opposition, of the American people. When the corporate-owned media characterize—as they invariably do—most efforts of a people to escape victimization as actions menacing to freedom, the interests served are those of private power centers.

CONCLUSION: TRANSNATIONAL IDEOLOGY AND PRESERVATION OF THE HUMAN COMMUNITY

In sum, the resources of the transnational corporate system, technological and legal, to say nothing of economic and military, are formidable. Yet when called upon, each element of power sets in motion a dynamic that reduces greatly the seeming omnipotence of the system. The dazzling communication technologies impose dependencies on their users. The resort to extraterritorial pressure encourages resistance at national and regional levels. The application of military force, if unlimited, is mutually self-destructive. Limited application often supplies the texts and hones the discipline for the next generation of freedom-fighters.

Still, it would be unrealistic to imagine that the reaction generated by the application of the power of the system would precipitate a crisis and an early demise of the transnational order. It still possesses enormous material and ideological power. Not least, in the latter category, is its talent for defining democracy and freedom as personal consumption, and claiming further that a standard of living is to be understood exclusively as an individual attainment, measured by the accumulation of material possessions.

Once this outlook is in place, in the conscious and unconscious minds of the citizenry, community values recede and the reverence for individual accumulation increasingly takes precedence over social needs and services, and over public well-being itself.

What, then, may be concluded from this review of the status of information produced by the transnational corporate system? In brief, the demand for a new international information order that has grown since the 1960s cannot be understood exclusively as a preoccupation with the direction of the message flow or even with the quality of the information passing through the circuits. These unquestionably are vital matters: the institutional configurations responsible for the existing inequalities and inadequacies must be confronted and changed. But they cannot be changed by the introduction of systems of advanced electronic information technology, at least not as they are presently administered. They can increase the volume of the flow and may even allow some two-way transmissions. *But, as they are currently organized, operated, and controlled, the high tech circuits and systems are the instrumentation with which place after place around the world is integrated into the transnational corporate business system. Unless we agree to have a "for sale" sign put on all human relationships, we must call the transnational system itself to account. This is the central issue, today and tomorrow.*

Because the new information technologies and the mass media provide the essential productive, organizational, and ideological underpinning of the TNCs, the confrontations looming in international communications may well be decisive in determining the shape and quality of human experience in the time ahead.

NOTES

1. See A. W. Singham, ed., *The Non-Aligned Movement in World Politics,* Westport, CT, Lawrence Hill and Co., 1977. Esp. Tran Van Dinh, "Non-Alignment and Cultural Imperialism."

2. By Kaarle Nordenstreng and Tapio Varis, Reports and Papers on Mass Communications, no. 7, UNESCO, Paris.

3. "Cultural Statements," Feb. 24. 1983.

4. See Claude Collomb, "1208 Télévisions privées en Italie," *Le Monde Dimanche,* Nov. 14, 1982.

5. Gerald Sussman, "Telecommunications Technology: Transnationalizing the New Philippine Information Order," *Media, Culture and Society,* 4 (1982): 51.

6. See Joëlle Stolz, "L'Algérie regarde 'Dallas,' " *Le Monde Dimanche,* Oct. 10, 1982, p. 1.

7. Caitlin Randall, "Peruvian TV Hoping to Emerge from Dark Ages," *Advertising Age,* Sept. 27, 1982.

8. "Le discours de Mexico," *Le Monde,* Aug. 7, 1982.

9. See "Culture: faut-il brûler les Américaines?" *Le Nouvelle Observateur,* Aug. 7, 1982.

10. "Eldorado in our Back Yard," *The Guardian,* Jan. 17, 1983.

11. *The Transnational Data Report* (July/Aug. 1982) notes: "Yielding to pressure from some national federations making up the Business and Advisory Council (BIAC) the OECD Expert Group on TDF has deleted this question (on the volume of internal, intracorporate computer-to-computer communications) on forms now being distributed to corporations in the 23 Member Countries. *TDR* understands that a number of companies consider this data as sensitive and proprietary. The OECD experts had wanted these details to help assess the importance and uses of TDF by multinational corporations" (p. 20). Also, a UNESCO study, *Transnational Communication and Cultural Industries* (Thomas Guback, Tapio Varis, et. al., Reports and Papers on Communication, UNESCO, Paris, 1982) notes: "There is so far no global inventory that gives quantitative and qualitative information on the TNCs in communication" (p.7).

12. An example of selling off public services to private profit-making enterprises was the Reagan administration plan to sell four weather satellites and a satellite for land resources surveying to private industry. See Philip M. Boffey, "Administration Proposes Selling U.S. Weather Satellites to Industry," *New York Times,* March 9, 1983, p. 1. For a more comprehensive background analysis of this development, see Herbert I. Schiller, *Who Knows: Information in the Age of the Fortune 500,* Norwood, N.J., Ablex, 1981, chap. 6, "Planetary Resource Information Flows: A New Dimension of Hegemonic Power or Global Social Utility?" See also Anita R. and Herbert I. Schiller, "Who Can Own What America Knows?" *The Nation,* April 17, 1982, and Herbert S. Dordick et. al., *The Emerging Network Marketplace,* Ablex, 1981.

13. Anthony Smith, *The Geopolitics of Information,* New York, Oxford University Press, 1980, p. 176.

14. Cees Hamelink, *Finance and Information,* Norwood, N.J., Ablex, 1983, p. 97.

15. Jeff Gerth, "Citicorp Maneuvers Called Questionable by U.S. Aide," *International Herald Tribune,* Sept. 14, 1982, p. 9.

16. "A Delivery that may be Dresser-France's Last," *Business Week,* Oct. 18, 1982, p. 50.

17. Bukassa Bukassa, "Zaire Grapples with Telematics," *Transnational Data Report,* vol. 5, no. 5 (July/Aug. 1982): 255-56.

18. Reported in the Document Service of the International Institute of Communication, Washington, D.C., Feb. 1983.

19. "Brazil: The Role of TNCs, TDF Impacts, and Effects of National Policies," *Transnational Data Report,* vol. 5, no. 7 (Oct./Nov. 1982): 329-35.

20. See *Radiofrequency Use and Management: Impacts from the World Administrative Radio Conference of 1979, Summary*, Office of Technology Assessment, Congres-

sional Board of the 97th Congress, Congress of the United States, Washington, D.C., 1980, pp. 8-9. The no-nonsense, straightforward comments of the study are worth quoting in detail:

"The world environment for telecommunications has changed significantly in recent years; two-thirds of the 155 member nations of ITU can be classified as developing or Third World countries. There were 65 nations and seven groups of colonies present at the 1947 Atlantic City Conference, 80 nations and five groups of colonies at the 1959 WARC, and 142 nations (no colonies) at WARC-79."

"There are basic differences between the United States and Third World countries over the principles that should govern the allocation and use of the radio spectrum and related satellite orbit capacity."

"Third World countries are increasingly able to influence and shape international communication policies in international forums."

"The United States must maintain its technological leadership and expand its influence if future actions in a 'one-nation-one-vote' forum like ITU are to be favorable to U.S. positions."

"There has been a gradual shift toward recognizing the legitimacy of nontechnical factors such as political and cultural interests and values in ITU deliberations and in other international forums."

"U.S. requirements for access to the frequency spectrum and geostationary satellite orbit locations are expanding with the explosive growth in telecommunications/information technology, the growing use of satellites, and the increasing dependence on radio and satellites for military and national security purposes."

"The disparity between nations in their ability to use the spectrum is growing: this leads to growing disagreement over the allocation and use of specific frequency bands for specific services."

"Spectrum decisions arrived at as a result of voting within the ITU, as opposed to the commonly practiced consensus approach, will tend to be increasingly adverse to the U.S."

21. Ibid., pp. 18-19.

22. Letter of the president of the United States to the speaker of the House of Representatives, Thomas P. O'Neill, Jr., Sept. 17, 1981.

23. An *International Herald Tribune* report, for example, headlined the UN declaration, "Third World, Soviet Block Uphold Veto of Satellite TV Broadcasts." A *New York Times* account also cast the UN action in a negative and restrictive light: "The General Assembly, endorsing a curb on the free flow of information, has declared, in effect, that all nations have the right to block television broadcasts coming by satellite from abroad" (*International Herald Tribune,* Nov. 24, 1982). See also Eric Pace, "UN General Assembly Endorses Curb on Satellite TV Broadcasts," *International Herald Tribune,* Dec. 13, 1982.

24. Douglas E. Rosenthal and William M. Knighton, *National Laws and International Commerce: The Problem of Extraterritoriality,* London, Routledge and Kegan Paul, 1982.

CHAPTER THREE

Women and NWICO

Margaret Gallagher

Up to 1975, the issues of the status of women and of the New World Information and Communication Order had scarcely surfaced in international debate. Yet the five years between 1975 and 1980 saw not simply their emergence but their establishment as two focal points of international concern. In many ways both issues owed their recognition, and indeed their definition—at least at the level of international politics—to analyses of another, still elusive, issue: the establishment of a New International Economic Order (NIEO).

By the end of the 1960s it was undeniable that dominant postwar models of development, based on a theory of economic growth linked to industrialization, urbanization, structural specialization, and the like, had failed the developing world. The models, Western-generated, were ethnocentric in their assumptions. In retrospect, their failure was inevitable. New models, whose premises underlie the call for a New International Economic Order, propose radical changes in both the existing international economic system and in the policies and plans of developing countries themselves.

In highlighting the increasing concentration of capital—and concomitant economic control—in a relatively small number of Western-based transnational enterprises, these new models of development direct attention toward modern versions of dependence. Their prognosis is a development based on autonomous and endogenous growth, leading to individual and collective self-reliance. Notions such as popular participation and equal access to resources and benefits are also close to the heart of such formulations.

The Declaration on the Establishment of a New International Economic Order was adopted by the United Nations General Assembly in 1974. The following year, at the World Conference for International Women's Year, held in Mexico City, the group of nonaligned countries (or group of 77 as it was then commonly known) introduced what was probably the most contentious item to be considered at the conference—the so-called Declaration of Mexico, which attributed women's unequal status to underdevelopment and linked the solution of the problem to a new and just international economic order.

WOMEN'S STATUS AND SOCIO-ECONOMIC DEFINITIONS

Women's socio-economic status in the world is indeed dire. By 1980 it could be summed up by the much-quoted but adroit statement: "while they represent 50 percent of the world adult population and one-third of the official labor force, [women] perform for nearly two-thirds of all working hours, receive only one-tenth of the world income, and own less than 1 percent of world property" (WCUNDW, 1980a para. 16). Women's political participation globally amounts to a median of 12 percent at local levels and just 6 percent at national levels (WCUNDW, 1980b, para. 19). Illiteracy affects 35 percent of the world female population, compared with 23 percent of the male (WCUNDW, 1980c, para. 86). In Africa, Asia, and the Arab states there is a difference of about 25 percentage points in the female-male illiteracy rates.

Far from showing any improvement, the gap between women and men is increasing annually (Scott, 1984). Some examples: in developed market economies the unemployment rate among young women grew at a faster rate than among young men during the 1970s (WCUNDW, 1980d, para. 54). In many countries of Asia and Latin America the percentage of women employed in the industrial sector has been falling, while that of men has been rising (ibid., para. 27-8); case studies of the introduction of "improved methods" in agriculture in Africa found that, though they decreased the burden of work for men, women's burden was increased (ibid., para. 12).

These growing disparities might seem paradoxical in the face of a burgeoning body of legislation on equal rights, or the proliferation of political institutions that now represent women's interests in many countries. In reality, the United Nations review of progress concluded, such mechanisms are undermined "by inadequate allocation of financial resources," reflecting "the priority governments accord to issues concerning women," and by "limited mandates" that "restrict them to welfare activities traditionally associated with women" (WCUNDW, 1980a, para. 18).

Strict controls dictate the terms of reference under which promotion of women's emancipation is permitted. In 1980, for example, it was reported that "in at least one country during the past year advisory and consultative bodies have been dissolved" when they "attempted to link women's problems with broader socio-economic issues beyond welfare concerns" (WCUNDW, 1980e, para. 29). They had "gone too far" in attempting to analyze and extend the circumscriptions of their allotted place (Morgan, 1978).

These recent legislative and institutional developments might fairly be regarded as mere elements in a strategy of containment. At their heart is a conceptualization of women that rests on an utterly androcentric view of the world, in which women are seen as a "minority" or "marginal" group. So predominant is the system of priorities and values within which this worldview is set that even minimal gestures to women's advancement can be held "responsible" for all manner of social problems.

For example, the economist Hans Below ascribes the "real causes of unemployment" in the Federal Republic of Germany to such protective measures as "maternity leave" and "rights for minorities" such as women and the disabled (Lebaube, p. 12); and this at a time when unemployment in Germany is already higher, and increasing more rapidly, among women than men (Eurostat, 1983). Below's conclusion rests on a structure of knowledge that interprets the world from a male perspective. It defines the problem of gender in a way that renders it insoluble.

WOMEN'S STATUS AND THE ROLE OF INFORMATION

Between 1975 and 1980 there was also an increasing recognition at the international level of the relationship between women's status and the role of information and communication. As early as 1975 the World Plan of Action adopted at the Mexico City conference characterized women's lack of control over, or even access to, communication channels as both a symptom and a cause of their disadvantaged position. In the succeeding five years the analysis was sharpened at a series of regional and international meetings. The result, spelled out in a paper prepared for the 1980 Mid-Decade Conference in Copenhagen, was a call for "international communication networks of and about women, to rectify an imbalance which is part of the world imbalance in communication" (WCUNDW, 1980f, para. 34). The Program of Action itself asks the United Nations and UNESCO to "ensure the inclusion of women in the current work undertaken in preparation for the new international information order as both recipients and participants in information systems in which their problems and issues are discussed" (WCUNDW 1980a, para. 265). Thus by 1980 analyses linked improvement in the status of women to the solution of two global problems: economic and information imbalance and dependency.

By 1980 also, of course, these two problems had themselves been analytically linked. The concept of a New World Information and Communication Order (NWICO), as it had by then become known, had been a decade in the making. Broadly speaking, it responded to concerns similar to those that had motivated the call for a new international economic order: a recognition of global imbalance (in this case, in the flow of information), of increasing concentration of communication resources in Western-based transnational agencies, and of the role of transnational communication in creating dependence while fostering consumption-oriented values. A new information order would be based on principles reminiscent of those underlying the NIEO endogenous growth: self-reliance, pluralism, participation, cooperation. Initially conceived as a major problem in itself, the communication imbalance was soon closely linked with the new international economic order.

Again the nonaligned countries played a central role in elaborating the linkage, most influentially at their symposium on communication issues held in Tunis in 1976. The linkage was expressed both casually and symptomatically, in an analysis strikingly similar to that seeking to explain the relationship between women and information-communication. The first point to be stressed was the power of the information and communication media to create attitudes either antagonistic or receptive to the tenets of the NIEO, and thus to impede or encourage its establishment. More fundamentally, the new information order came to be seen as an integral element of the new economic order, in the sense that information had itself become a valuable economic commodity and resource. For example, according to Tom McPhail, "now more than 50 percent of the U.S. gross national product relates to information-based services" (McPhail, p. 32). Seen in this light, lack of control over modern means of communication implied vulnerability not simply to cultural imperialism, but to yet another facet of outright economic domination. (These interrelationships are fully explored in Pavlic and Hamelink, 1982.)

The link between economic and information imbalances was first officially recognized by the international community in the Declaration on the Mass Media, adopted by the UNESCO General Conference in 1978 (specifically in Articles VI and VII of the Declaration). By 1980, both the MacBride Report and (though more obliquely) the objectives of the International Program for the Development of Communication—the two major substantive outcomes of the international debate of the 1970s on information and communication—evidenced the extent to which interrelationships between the two concepts had been underwritten.

Yet in none of these documents does the other issue—that status of women—surface in more than a rudimentary way. The Mass Media Declaration, although explicit on the role of the media vis-à-vis the young (Article IV), ignores women altogether. The MacBride Report devotes two of its 250 substantive pages and one of its 82 recommendations to women's communication rights and needs. This is indeed curious, even paradoxical. The relevance of both NIEO and the NWICO had been debated and recognized in several international forums.

On the specific question of information and communication, in the years 1975 to 1980 the United Nations system had commissioned three international studies on women and the communication media (Ceulemans and Fauconnier, 1979; Gallagher, 1979; Cuevas, 1980). It had sponsored or co-sponsored at least twelve regional and international meetings on the theme; each meeting had produced a written report. In many of these there is ample evidence of discussion of the issues at the heart of the international debate on economic and information imbalances: underrepresentation, marginalization, distortion, access, and control. Evidently the two sets of discussions—one focused on women (including the women/communication relationship), the other on NWICO—were carried out simultaneously and voiced parallel concerns. But they remained, in the true manner of parallels, continuously equidistant.

A closer examination of some of the points of correspondence—underlying both the general foundation of NWICO and the specific problems affecting the relationship of women to information and communication—should help to explain the paradox raised by the fact that the two debates never actually intersected. It should also highlight some basic questions about the conceptual and political underpinnings of each.

COMMUNICATING THE STATUS OF WOMEN

The entire structure, organization, and output of the communication and information industries reflect, feed, and perpetuate a worldview in which women and women's interests are subordinate. My own recent research into the employment of women in television in EEC member states indicates that, although many broadcasting organizations have formally acknowledged women's claim for equal rights—even, in some cases, to the extent of proclaiming "equal opportunity" policies—women's jobs are still vertically and horizontally segregated so severely that women media workers, as a group, are virtually powerless. The "education system" and "trade-union power" are cited to explain why the situation is outside the control of the organizations themselves. The "economic recession" explains why no positive change-oriented measures can be initiated.

Thames Television sees itself "at the forefront of the development of Equal Opportunities in the United Kingdom" (in a recent job advertisement). Indeed, it is almost unique among the organizations I studied in that it has a budget item for the promotion of equality. Yet the total budget for 1984—and it is expected to promote both race *and* sex equality—amounts to the approximate production costs of two 30-minute situation comedy programs (Gallagher, 1984).

In terms of content, it is not simply what the media say, or how they say it, that bolsters stereotypical, limited, and skewed perceptions of women (see Gallagher, 1981, for a synthesis of worldwide research on this issue). Equally important is what they do *not* say. As an example, look at a *Washington Post* editorial from January 1983. Entitled "America's Dispossessed," it examines the plight of the unemployed. Starting with the question "Why can't these people find work" it states that some U.S. workers who were driven to take menial jobs that are usually the reserve of "illegal immigrants and other fringe members of society," had given them up within a few days. The explanation:

> Low pay and harsh working conditions were part of the reason. But so was self-respect. . . . Minimum level wages are now derided as "women's pay." Perhaps that attitude partly explains why women haven't been hit

as hard by this recession as men have. But before you prescribe a steady diet of minimum wages for the unemployed, remember that . . . a minimum-wage worker clears less than $6,000 a year, far below the official poverty level for a family of four. Try providing food, clothing, housing and medical care for a family on that . . . and you'll see why breadwinners can't settle for it [reprinted in *The Guardian Weekly,* Jan. 16, 1983].

Ostensibly about unemployment, the editorial is actually about *male* unemployment. Reading it we could not guess that the unemployment rate for women in the United States is higher than that for men (WCUNDW, 1980d, para. 62). Instead, we learn that women's lack of self-respect means they will accept low pay and harsh working conditions. This leads to the apparently value-based conclusion that "women haven't been hit as hard by this recession as men have." (In fact, a 1984 study by the Congressional Research Service shows that women-headed families have suffered most in the U.S. recession: Pear, p. 3). Of course the editorial equates "breadwinners" with "men," whose family responsibilities mean they "can't settle" for the minimum wage. It ignores the fact that by the late 1970s, 14 percent of all families in the U.S.A. were headed by women (WCUNDW, 1980d, para. 82), and that about one-third of such families were below the poverty level, compared with about one-twentieth of male-headed families (ibid., para. 92).

The tone of the editorial is one of near contempt for women's apparent willingness to accept menial jobs, harsh working conditions, and the derisory minimum wage, and of approval for men's self-respect, which leads them not to settle for these. The circumstances that lead to the different responses of women and men are not questioned, much less challenged. The editorial speaks for the same perspective as Hans Below's casting women as "fringe members" of a world in which their aspirations and, therefore, their rewards are "naturally" subordinate to those of men.

WOMEN'S STATUS AND COMMUNICATION SYSTEMS: STRUCTURAL RELATIONSHIPS

This perspective can be set in a more properly global framework by an analysis of some of the structural relationships between women's status and communication systems. In the first place, at the level of global information and economic flows, women are a central—perhaps even a focal—part of the processes involved in transnationalization.

The role played by the transnationals has become a central focus of the debates on international economic and information flows. The MacBride Report underscored two aspects of their influence. First, "not only do these conglomerates mobilize capital and technologies and transfer them to the communication market; they also market countless socio-cultural consumer goods which serve as a vehicle for an amalgam of ideas, tastes, values, and beliefs." Secondly, it went on, "the transnational exerts a direct influence on the economic production apparatus of the countries in which they operate" (MacBride, p. 38). Taking each of these aspects in turn I hope to show how, at the level of global information and economic systems, women are a central—perhaps even a focal—part of the processes of transnationalization at issue.

Global Issues

In the industrialized world, women, for at least the past fifty years, have been the prime target for advertisers and marketers of consumer goods. Christine Frederick's book in which the doctrine of the "consumer society" was first elaborated, aptly entitled *Selling Mrs. Consumer,* was published in 1929. Even earlier, at the end of the nineteenth century, J. Walter Thompson had been the first to seize on women's magazines as the most efficient and effective means of reaching a vast market: as J. W. T. was fond of reciting, "women spend the money" (Mattelart, p. 44).

In an extraordinary and continuing process, first in the United States but soon spreading to Western Europe, particular images of women—the efficient housewife, caring wife and mother, wise manager of household budget, elegant beauty, modern superwoman organizing a "double-day," liberated sophisticate—to which the mass of women were expected to respond, were developed in the media (in particular, in women's magazines). The marketing strategy, according to which women were encouraged to adopt the roles and the consumer goods associated with the various images, was complex; but it was successful. The entire process, its demands on women, and its successive adaptations to the fluctuating requirements of modern capital expansion, have been analyzed in several studies (for example, Ewen, 1976; Mattelart, 1981).

The process is persistently adaptive, its protagonists self-styled duck-hunters who know that "the way to hit a target is to aim at where it's going to be, not at where it's been" (Bartos, p. 290). Among J. W. T.'s "ducks" for the 1980s are the professional executive woman and woman heads of households. The "professional executive" now constitutes a sufficiently important market for *Newsweek* to be published in a special edition for women readers, to streamline its appeal to "advertisers who want to reach this particular segment" (Bartos, p. 288). As for women who head their own households, although they are "fairly poor," they "may be a growing market" (ibid., p. 93).

More recently, the search for new markets in the developing world has seen the beginning of a similar process here too. Again, women are a central target in the bid to create "modern" (read "consumer-oriented") aspirations. Again, magazines are the primary—though by no means the only—vehicle. Often such magazines are transnational products, edited and produced outside the countries in which they are distributed, with perhaps some superficial "adaptation" to local customs and style. One example is *Amina,* edited and produced in France, and distributed throughout francophone Africa. Its advertising, almost exclusively for beauty and fashion items, directs readers to French mail-order businesses or publicizes the products of transnational firms. The "model" of beauty and glamor it proposes to its readers is unarguably Western. (See Santa Cruz and Erazo, pp. 126–27, for a vivid pictorial illustration of this point.)

In Kenya in 1983, advertisements for Clear-Tone—a skin cream produced by West German-based Nicholas Laboratories, one of the top ten advertising spenders in Kenya—were informing women that "in London, Paris, and New York, the beautiful people have one thing in common, a beautiful skin." These cities constitute the "fresh, young world of Clear-Tone. Where beautiful skin is in." To be "in" and part of this "world," the inference goes, buy Clear-Tone.

A similar role is played in Latin America by magazines such as *Vanidades, Cosmopolitan,* and *Buenhogar* ("good housekeeping"), controlled by giant transnationals such as the Hearst Corporation. Almost a third of the space in these magazines is devoted to advertising. One 1977 study of these three transnational magazines—as well as of fifteen national magazines—in Brazil, Mexico, Colombia, Venezuela, and Chile, found that 60 percent of *all* advertisements (i.e., across both transnational *and* national magazines) were for products of transnational enterprises; the majority of them were for beauty or fashion articles, followed by items for use in the home (Santa Cruz and Erazo, ibid.).

If the middle-class, literate woman in rapidly developing countries has been especially singled out as a vessel for change, the enormous mass of women—poor, illiterate—in less developed areas do not escape either: they too are vessels, and more clearly victims of changing patterns. There is probably no need to dwell on the disastrous effects of distorted advertising by transnational firms eager to "off-load" products—powdered baby food, contraceptives—for which markets can no longer be found in the industrialized world. Instances are by now well known.

Less clearly recognized, and a point developed by Michele Mattelart, are the implications of the advertising methods used by these firms. The marketing of their products depends at least partly on their being situated in and associated with a particular vision of progress, of modernization. In buying such things, the suggestion is that you buy a part of modern life; in other words, when you buy and use these products, you become connected with another—"modern"—world. This approach reverberates with echoes of the exogenous development models rejected in the call for a new international economic order. It promises modernization without providing the conditions on which "modern" practices—such as the use of powdered baby food—are contingent: in this case, for example, access to fresh water and to hygienic equipment, knowledge of babies' nourishment needs, understanding of measurement principles, and so on. Its appeal to women rests on the creation of a worldview in which modernity becomes a value to which all women may and should aspire. It is an appeal whose noxious philosophy is transparent in the advice given to businesses specializing in the sale of foodstuffs in a 1978 issue of *Business International*:

Aim your advertising at women, the main customers. Make the product known, and develop a desire for the brand, without recourse to words—in regions where illiteracy is widespread a drawing or a brand symbol can be a great help. Try to give your products a Western look, a sign of social status in rapidly developing areas where ideas of modernization and Westernization are closely associated [quoted in Mattelart, p. 54].

Women, from the most to the least developed parts of the world, have become a fulcrum for the interpenetration of transnational economics and communication, in exactly the manner suggested by the first part of the extract quoted earlier from the MacBride Report. Turning briefly to the second statement in that extract—concerning the influence of the transnationals on the economic production apparatus of countries—there is ample evidence that women are of the utmost importance here too. They constitute a key resource in the international division of labor. Without dwelling on the point, it is significant that women account for almost 90 percent of the unskilled workforce in transnational electronics firms in Central and Latin America and in Southeast Asia, where the large, unorganized, and poorly paid female labor force is highly vulnerable to exploitation (WCUNDW, 1980g). Recruitment of young women from rural areas uses methods strikingly similar to the strategies already described in the marketing of consumer goods:

Recruiting officers will glorify the . . . working environment (complete with piped music, cool, air-conditioned, and dust-free shops). . . . Associated benefits such as . . . beauty-grooming classes, annual dinners, talent-time and beauty contests are always highlighted. . . . In addition, these young rural women are deliberately led to think that going to work in electronics factories in the city is also a means to gain Western culture and modern ideas" [*From Struggling to Survive: Women Workers in Asia,* quoted in *ISIS International Bulletin,* 24 (1981) 13.]

The reality is altogether different. Lim (1980), Ehrenreich and Fuentes (1981), and Heyzer (1982) document the appalling work conditions and triple-level exploitation that are the reality.

It is remarkable that this entire phenomenon has been largely ignored by the media, both transnational and national. It has been left to the feminist press—for example, *Spare Rib, Ms. Magazine, ISIS*—to lay bare and analyze the roots of the problem. The only item I have come across in the "mainstream" media is apparently motivated by the news that "after years of being a nearly all-female preserve, Mexico's border assembly plants have begun to employ men" (Meislin, p. 11).

This brings up two fundamental questions that must be faced in trying to explain the relationship between women and information—whether as conceived in terms of the old order or of the new. One question, which will be tackled later, concerns the criteria and definitions that make an issue "newsworthy," given that existing definitions apparently exclude many aspects of life that are of paramount importance to women. The second question—whose prior consideration is essential to analysis of the first—raises the matter of whose interests are being served in these various presences and absences of women in the international flow of capital and communication.

It would be difficult to argue that women benefit. It is tempting to see the beneficiaries as none other than the impersonal, corporate interests of transnational enterprises. But it is impossible to ignore the role of national governments, or indeed that of international agencies such as the World Bank, in collaborating with or promoting transnational interests—and thus in underwriting the exploitation of women. (See Siegel, 1978, Ehrenreich and Fuentes, 1981, for more detailed treatment of this point.) The silence of national media on these problems—indeed their collaboration in the creation of restricted and stereotyped images of women—becomes more understandable.

Commenting on this very problem, Breda Pavlic and Cees Hamelink suggest that "the link between the mass media, the governments, and private enterprises (TNEs or other) is much stronger than the defenders of the 'free press' (and opponents of NWICO and NIEO) would like one to think" (Pavlic and Hamelink, p. 79). It becomes quite clear that among the principal *supporters* of the new orders are countries in which this very link—between media, government, and private enterprises—is absolutely evident in relation to their exploitation of women in the ways just discussed. We are here entering some of the deepest and muddiest waters of international politics; although relevant to the theme of this paper, it cannot be its proper focus. There is, however, one other important point to be considered, relating to interest groups.

Examining the mechanisms used by transnational enterprises to exploit women workers in Central America and Southeast Asia, Barbara Ehrenreich and Annette Fuentes demonstrate that identical practices are used by private enterprises *within* the United States. Small assembly plants, staffed almost entirely by women—often single mothers and heads of households—forced to "moonlight" in order to make ends meet, operate in contempt of all legislation at slave-labor rates of pay. Much evidence could be cited of economic discrimination against women throughout the industrialized world. (See, for example, the United Nations report *The Economic Role of Women in the EEC Region,* 1980.) Such testimony indicates that the ideology underlying the existing economic order is not simply capitalist. It is also blatantly sexist—a point all too readily buried or ignored in international discussions. This will be taken up again, below.

So far, I have tried to outline some of the strands that come together to bind women to the most central processes of global economic and communication systems. In these processes, women are primarily a *resource,* whose function may vary but whose character does not—central, yet peripheral; object, rather than subject; acted on, rather than participant. The central presence of this woman-resource in the processes, and yet apparent absence form the official formulation of the problems posed by the processes, must raise doubts about the balance between rhetoric and reality in the calls for a new international order. These doubts gain even more substance when analysis shifts to the level of national economic and information systems. At this level the women/media relationship is almost an analogue of the international communication scene.

National Issues

There are two recognized dimensions to the international imbalance in the flow and content of information: the quantitative and the qualitative. Tom McPhail summarizes them:

> Two complaints commonly crop up concerning the news that the Big Four [news agencies] report about the LDCs. For one, there is simply not enough of it. . . . The other criticism . . . is that what there is of it tends to be sensationalistic, insensitive to the goals and values of the LDCs, and distorted, usually by the application of Western stereotypes, biases, norms, cultural perspectives, and even ideological designs about the nations and materials being covered [McPhail, pp. 175-76].

Turning immediately to another summary—this time by Marilee Karl, who describes the general research findings concerning presentation of women by the media in both industrialized and developing countries—we find a remarkable similarity in the stated problems:

1. Women are virtually absent from the "important" news of the world, whether transmitted by press, radio, or television.
2. Very little media coverage is given to women's work, achievements, situations, or needs.
3. The media are responsible for perpetuating and disseminating traditional stereotypes of women.
4. When women are involved in organizing and action, and especially when they step out of their traditional roles, the media often distort and ridicule.
5. Women lack access to information they need and to which they have a right, information which would help them answer questions affecting their daily lives, problems, and needs [Karl, p. 27].

If, in McPhail's summary, we substitute "women" for "LDCs" and "male-controlled/male" for "Big Four/Western," we might almost be reading another version of Karl's summary. As Karl aptly points out, "the one characteristic of present information structures which is rarely mentioned, but which has far-reaching consequences, is that they are male-dominated" (ibid., p. 26).

This is not a resort to obscurantism. It does not deny the correctness of the criticisms of the North-South flow. But it does argue that a completely parallel set of criticisms refers to imbalances—not simply in the global system itself, but *within all national communication systems*—that cast women and men in a dependency relationship very similar to that between developing and industrialized countries. (This point is argued, with specific reference to economic relationships, in Leghorn and Parker, pp. 207-10.)

Let me take up and briefly develop the points in Marilee Karl's summary. In the interests of brevity I shall confine the discussion to the treatment of women in the news, although most of the points apply equally to *all* aspects of media content.

First, women rarely appear in news coverage. Studies carried out in quite different countries underline this basic absence. For example, in 1979 women constituted only 8 percent of newsmakers across eighteen main newspapers monitored in Sri Lanka (Goonatilake, 1980). Studies of the main U.S. network television news programs carried out for the United States Commission on Civil Rights found that the percentage of women in newsmaking roles actually fell between 1975 and 1977—from 14 to 7 percent (U.S. Commission on Civil Rights, 1979). Other studies report gross underrepresentation of women in the news media of, for example, Tanzania (Kyaruzi, 1979), Hungary (Hanak, 1982), Ireland (Working Party on Women in Broadcasting, 1981), and Canada (Robinson, 1978). Still other research attests to trivialized or sensationalized treatment of those women who *are* portrayed in the news (Karl's third point): for example, in Australia (Women Media Workers, 1978), Japan (Ide, 1978), Zambia (Glazer Schuster, 1979), Austria (Arbeitsgruppe Frauenmaul, 1979). Many other studies could be cited, and there is no particular significance attached to those mentioned other than that they illustrate how the problem is not confined to any particular type of national economic system or to any particular part of the world.

Many of the factors that influence coverage (or noncoverage) of women equally affect other social groups at the margins of national power structures: "event-oriented" reporting, emphasis on political and economic elites, the "beat" structure in news gathering, responsiveness to public visibility. However, there is one overarching factor that has particular implications for women as a group: the fact that most news reporters and editors are *men*. In 1977 only about 15 percent of print journalists in Norway, Denmark, and the Federal Republic of Germany were women (Marzolf, 1977). In Pakistan and southern India women represented no more than 3 percent of print journalists (Habib, 1980; Chabbra, 1980). In 1980, just 14 percent of news reporters and 6 percent of current-affairs producers in BBC television were women (Baehr, 1980). In Japan, NHK has recruited no women news reporters for twenty years, and women print journalists are about 1 percent of the total (Nuita, 1979). Again, the figures are no more than a selection. But they illustrate that, from one country to another, the world of news selection and reporting is a masculine world.

It seems inevitable, then, that this selection and reporting will reflect a male ordering of priorities—that there will be issues and areas of life that go completely unnoticed. As the first woman to head a *New York Times* bureau commented, "There have been times when I found editors unaware of things happening, like the rape laws. Only women think in terms of rape laws; the men know about capital punishment" (quoted in Tuchman, 1978). Not only may women-related concerns and activities be ignored but, if covered, they may suffer from biased or distorted reporting (points two and four in Karl's summary).

For example, Gertrude Robinson concludes that news coverage of the women's movement in the United States has gone through three distinct stages, relating to the stages of growth of the movement itself. A "news blackout" in the first years (1966-1969), when the activities of the embryonic movement were ignored, was followed by a "sanitization" phase corresponding to the growing organizational power of the movement (1970-1972). During this phase ridicule and sensationalist reporting (for example, featuring bra-burning—something that never actually took place) went hand in hand with soft pedalling on issues such as inequalities in pay, employment, and so on. Once the movement was established (after 1973, when the National Organization of Women had 40,000 members and a budget of half a million dollars), a third period began in which a limited amount of serious coverage, although assured, was continually undermined by being accorded low prestige and by trivialization (Robinson, pp. 98-102). News items buried away at the end of a bulletin or on the final inside pages of a newspaper tell the public clearly that this is not "important" news.

Language is a powerful tool in news presentation. We are well accustomed to the term "women's libber"—indeed it may seem rather "cute." The impossibility of describing a member of the PLO as a "Palestinian libber" or of FRELIMO as a "Mozambican libber" is a forceful reminder of how desperately pernicious this particular media technique—trivialization and ridicule—is to women aiming at a change.

Various analyses of women and the media have suggested that the major solution to these problems is to ensure that more professional women penetrate decision-making areas within the media (Butler and Paisley, 1980). But the answers are not so simple. A myriad of factors—institutional, structural, social, professional—conspire to ensure that most media women, like most media men, will operate within an identical ideological paradigm. For example, after a screening of advertisements à la J. Walter Thompson, showing women exclusively in traditional roles, a management male commented that many of the ads were written by women. A female senior vice-president with the company reports: "I answered that they weren't writing as women, they were writing as professionals. And they were working within a given strategy" (Bartos, p. 243; see also Tuchman, 1978, for a good account of many of these difficulties).

The complexity of the problem is, however, gaining recognition. As an illustration, the most recent task force to report on Canadian broadcasting went beyond simple calls for more female staff appointments, and asked for representation for "feminist organizations" (on an advisory committee) and for appointment of "individuals conversant with problems of sex-role stereotyping and the portrayal of women" (quoted in *Media Report to Women,* p. 9).

Finally (and touching on Marilee Karl's last summary point), to indicate some of the ways in which certain women *do* actually conceive of, organize, and execute their work differently from men—while still experiencing many of the problems already mentioned—I shall refer in some detail to a recent study of Danish television news journalists (Jensen, 1982). Else Jensen interviewed all women reporters and producers working in Danish television news in the autumn of 1980, and observed their work for a two-week period in early 1981. Women constituted 21 percent of the total news staff.

Taking foreign news first, Jensen found that it was heavily dominated by male newsmakers (91 percent), most of them heads of state, government spokesmen, or leaders of political organizations. One-fifth of all foreign news items were produced by women and of these *half* concerned the Third World (compared with 17 percent of male-produced foreign items). This is what Jensen has to say about treatment of the foreign news issues:

> There was a general tendency for the male journalist to discuss the issues on a strictly political level, whereas the women often considered the aspect of which *consequences* the exercise of power would actually have on the population [p. 14].

Domestic news items were also dominated by male newsmakers (86 percent). But half of the news items that *did* feature women were produced by female journalists. The other half were produced by two or three male journalists. Recalling the proportion of female to male journalists (20:80), it is evident that women journalists are much more likely to seek out women contributors. Jensen points out that this entails a departure from traditional journalistic conceptions of what is important news. "None of the female contributors was of interest in terms of traditional news, most of them were not known to the public beforehand, and they usually had a low status in the social hierarchy" (p. 19).

This raises another practical problem. Because they are not "known" figures, such contributors need a comparatively lengthy introduction in the bulletin. This bites into an already brief news item—another reason why it is "easier" to choose well-known figures, who will of course tend to be male. To choose to include a woman contributor, therefore, is a departure not just from traditional conceptions of news but from efficient reporting practice.

Although Jensen found that both male *and* female journalists contribute to a general mystification and abstraction—rather than clarification—of issues, she contends that there is a difference in their styles of presentation. She describes these as based on symbols of authority (male presentations: preference for studio-based, desk reporting) and authenticity (female presentation:

preference for on-the-spot reporting, with greater use of documentary material and interviews). She concludes:

> On a small scale, the women also turn their attention to viewpoints other than the traditional—in order to present the news in a more down-to-earth manner, and in order to cover issues which are more specific and closer to everyday life: this goes for conditions both at home and abroad [p. 20].

This brings out the female journalists' own predispositions. For most of them, it seems, "soft" news was synonymous with what they regarded as positive about their work, yet were often unable to report. Jensen grouped their self-reported work strategies into three clusters:

1. To accept that women are best at covering certain areas, which if not covered by women will remain untouched;
2. Consciously to depart from the traditional pattern and go for new topics which have hitherto been closed country to women, in order to prove to themselves and other women that this is actually possible;
3. To aim at greater valuation for the topics traditionally covered by women and to fight for a redefinition of other topics, to make them more representative of women's reality [pp. 7-8].

All three strategies speak to the conflict experienced by women working in the predominantly male environment of the media today. As Jensen points out, the initiatives being taken by the women she studied were at the *individual* level, in the face of a system that made such initiatives both daunting and difficult.

Of the three strategies, the last is certainly the most radical, but perhaps also the most difficult to implement. In its way too, it is the most redolent of the goals associated with a New World Information and Communication Order, which, it was agreed at a 1976 international seminar, must promote "another information, one which will fight preconceived ideas, ignorance, and alienation, and facilitate the 'conscientization' of citizens to ensure their control over decision-making" (quoted in Pavlic and Hamelink, pp. 27-28). And, recalling still other aspects of the strategies noted in Jensen's study of women journalists, the passage continues: "Change will require major conceptual and practical advances in both the content and methods of information, since the relationship between the 'professional' and the 'public' is also one of subservience" (Pavlic and Hamelink, p. 38).

Women: Central and Peripheral to Communication and Change

Even this limited presentation must have made it clear that women are absolutely central to the processes and inequalities at issue in the NWICO debate. They are a focus and a resource in the operations of transnational economics and communication. They exemplify fully, in their relation to both transnational *and* national media systems, the very problems that instigated the call for a new international order. Yet they are resoundingly absent from the NWICO conceptual framework and from the plans for its implementation.

This absence cannot be accidental, a mere oversight. We are coming to the end of the United Nations Decade for Women with its attendant flurry of women-related activity, much of it directly concerned with media, information, and communication. Nor can the absence be explained away as insignificant, in arguments maintaining that women as a group do not need specific mention or consideration, inasmuch as plans for social and structural change include *all* persons, both men *and* women. Such apparently philanthropic arguments are actually specious—at best unperceptive, at worst misogynist. They entirely ignore the weight of evidence that points to the specific aspect of *gender* in accounts of women's persistent, disadvantaged status across societies and through history. They completely disregard the particular problems faced by women as *women*—and not just as members of a social group or class, or as citizens of the industrialized or developing world—vis-à-vis information and communication.

To begin to explain the absence, in current formulations and plans for a new international order, of any dimension or perspective that truly takes account of the situation, rights and needs of women, it is enough to return to the analysis of the relationship of women to information and communication. The conclusion was that women are constituted as a resource in processes over which they have little or no control. As a corollary of this lack of control, they have no access to communication that could change the processes in which they are involved.

Within existing communication structures, although individual women may work for—and even bring about—change, these structures remain under the direction of men. Women are almost always extremely dependent on men—whether in governments, in private enterprises, in international agencies, in communication systems—*allowing* them to define problems, pursue policies, allocate resources, implement programs, in ways that would benefit women as a group. This is, evidently, a political problem.

To see how some of these mechanisms of control exclude women from the direction of change, I return to two major recent "events" of particular relevance to women and to NWICO—the Mid-Decade Conference on Women, and the MacBride Report.

The issue of communication could have been expected to figure at least to some extent at the 1980 Intergovernmental Conference in Copenhagen. The regional preparatory meetings for the conference had all stressed its importance. Three separate documents on the topic were prepared, one being the report and recommendations of an international seminar, described as a sectoral meeting for the conference and held at United Nations headquarters in New York just two months beforehand. Yet there was little or no discussion of communication at the Intergovernmental Conference. The proposals on communication in the Draft Program of Action were weak. At least two attempts to strengthen them ran aground because of governmental reluctance to become embroiled with issues that by 1980 had become highly controversial.

The tension between women's and governmental interests was highly visible throughout the conference. Its agenda (in terms of issues that were and were not emphasized), despite all the preparatory meetings and the detailed documentation, was—to use a term of compromise that became significant in conference discussions—*de facto* revised and reset by men.

A distinct "women's perspective" was noticeably absent at Copenhagen. Leaving aside the overt politicization in which sessions were disrupted by walkouts, or suspended by the use of committee tactics to prevent certain speakers from taking the floor, the dominant male perspective was at its most blatant in the debate on the causes of women's inequality. Again this was reduced to an *aspect* of general underdevelopment, itself caused by colonialism, neocolonialism, racism, imperialism, apartheid, zionism, and so on.

The attempt to introduce the concept of sexism as an additional—not to say overarching—factor led to an acrimonious debate, and resulted in the following compromise sentence: "The unfavorable status of women is *aggravated* in many countries, developed and developing, by *de facto* discrimination on the grounds of sex"; a footnote added that "in a group of countries [this is] called sexism" (WCUNDW, 1980a, para. 12; emphasis added).

The entire debate—in which half the speakers were men, a proportion well in excess of their representation at the conference—was trivializing and indeed insulting to women. (See Gallagher, 1981, pp. 159-63, for further discussion of these events.) Many of the women delegates—although by no means all to whom I spoke personally—were distressed and embarrassed by what was happening. But they could do almost nothing about it. They took their instructions from their governments.

The International Commission for the Study of Communication Problems (the MacBride Commission) began work in December 1977, when the UN Decade for Women was two years old. No woman was nominated to serve on the original 16-member commission; but when one of the original members withdrew, he was replaced by Betty Zimmerman, at that time director of Radio Canada International. It was in large part due to the efforts of Betty Zimmerman that women received any mention in the final report. One hundred papers were specially prepared at the request of the commission. Only one dealt with the issue of women (Gallagher, 1980). Its preparation was not requested until the spring of 1979; the commission met for the final time in November of that year.

The MacBride Report deals with women in a way that betrays this last-minute "grafting." A serious analysis of the problem might have led to some detailed discussion of women in the context, for example, of transnationalization, of advertising, of the formation of public opinion, of infrastructures, of professional communicators. But there is none. Instead, the "issue" of women is collapsed into two pages on "equal rights for women," which sit somewhat uneasily in a chapter entitled "Images of the World." It is difficult to interpret the entire episode as anything other than ill-disguised tokenism. If it were something else—belated realization of an important issue, or lack of data or expertise to deal with the implications raised—one could have expected the "women's issue" to be included in the final section of the report, entitled "Issues Requiring Further Study." But it does not.

These two accounts begin to show how far women are from being able to influence change. Even in situations where women are actually numerically superior, and much more obviously in those in which they fill the "statutory woman" criterion, the *directioning* of change remains a male monopoly.

For women there is little change. The Copenhagen Conference, whose main purpose was to review changes since 1975, reported little improvement and even some deterioration in the situation of women. Least improvement was found in the sphere of female participation in planning and decision-making, including that of the UN system itself.

Naomi Black, reviewing recent international activities related to women, concludes that "what has happened is that the international system has finally noticed the potential instrumental role of women in development" (Black, p. 273). In other words, women have been recognized as a development *resource*.

It is difficult to disagree with this view, which can be supported by countless statements about women and development in international documents. Even the Declaration on the Elimination of Discrimination against Women (adopted by the UN General Assembly in 1967) tells us that women's participation in all spheres of life is "a necessity for the full and complete development of a country." It seems that the *country* is meant to benefit, rather than women themselves. And indeed this is often the case, as an analysis of the results of projects aimed at the "integration of women in development" makes all too clear.

Increasingly, research is documenting how development projects—income-generating and family planning projects in particular—have actually worsened the situation of women in many cases. (See, for example, Rogers, 1980; Black and Cottrell, 1981.) New models of development may be less ethnocentric but they are no less androcentric.

Reduction of the "women's issue" to "a problem of underdevelopment which exists mainly as a result of unjust economic relations" (WCUNDW, 1980a, para. 3) is a sleight of hand that, whatever other interests it may serve, clearly does not address the interests of women. It completely conceals the deep structure of gender relationships worldwide. No change in the international balance of economics or communication will automatically transform them. Thelma McCormack, in her review of development theories, reminds us of this when she points out that most theories of development have had nothing to say about women. Arguing from the point that the problems of women in industrialized countries are "analytically important because they illustrate how a patriarchal system mediates modernization," she concludes that "modernization" has not eliminated women's inequality but simply "modernized" it (McCormack, 1981, pp. 17–18).

The same point was eloquently made by a leading Caribbean woman activist, Peggy Antrobus, at the Copenhagen Conference. She said:

> In Mexico [at the 1975 Conference] the issue of integrating women in development seemed clear. Now after five years I'm not so certain as I was, [because] as far as I'm concerned there are very few "developed countries." . . . Do we want to be integrated into "patriarchal development"? The goal of a feminist development strategy would be . . . to allow women to make decisions and to shape the societies in which they lived [quoted in Black, p. 265].

The stated principles of the new international order should allow women to do exactly that. Like the recruitment techniques of the transnational electronics firms, the promise and the reality may not correspond.

AN ISSUE IN ITS OWN RIGHT

A feminist approach to the study of the global problems argues that there is an identifiable women's perspective on all global issues, and that it is obscured by the structural relationships embedded in the gender problem itself. It is not an "aspect" or a "dimension" of other global problems, although it is commonly held to be so. This dominant, sterile interpretation—viewing the issue solely *in relation to* other, supposedly "wider" concerns, rather than as an issue *in its own right*—does not define the problem. It instead refracts its specific roots, history, and exigencies through a male-designed prism. The effective result is reinforcement of the status quo.

With the balance of power, in political, economic, and also intellectual terms, so skewed toward a male-originated set of models, women's emancipation has been defined for them as a more comprehensive "integration" into an existing structure. This is a gradualist approach; it sees women's advancement as a modest and dispersed scaling of ladders, when and where an expanding economy permits. In practice, a powerful battery of instruments—from financial restraints, occupational and educational segregation, through language and ideology, to various forms of violence—are used not only to constrain women, but also to explain why there is little or no improvement in their situation, "yet."

WOMEN AND THE COMPOSITION OF KNOWLEDGE, INFORMATION, AND COMMUNICATION

Communication media transmit information and images that reflect a gender bias. Communication research transmits ideas. Historically, women have not been participants in the construction of knowledge, any more than they have had access to mass communication channels. For example, a glance through volumes 1 to 3 of the *Mass Communication Review Yearbook* shows that only 7 percent of the single-author papers were written by women, and that women contributed to just 15 percent of all the published papers. Only one of these (McCormack, 1980) could be said to reflect a distinctive women's perspective.

Volume 4 of the *Yearbook* (1983) contains four female-authored papers in a section called "Feminism and Media." Unfortunately, this sectionalization obscures the relationship of these papers to other issues—particularly culture, policy, and structure—covered in the volume. Mary Evans points to the repercussions of such partitioning when she says that the general field of women's studies—and its practitioners—are "in an outer courtyard, far removed from the real centers of academic power and authority" in British and North American universities (Evans, p. 228).

Not only are universities and research institutes still largely male domains (for example, in 1984, less than a quarter of the members of the International Association of Mass Communication Researchers were women), but research topics, research policies, theoretical concepts, and research methodology all display male preoccupations and predilections. Although it has become less unusual for new academic publications to refer to the issues raised by the women's movement, such allusions are generally either made "in passing" (Galtung, p. 166; Worsley, p. 337) or are developed from such an androcentric perspective (Willetts, pp. 5 and 199–200) as to reinforce inveterate interpretations.

Until very recently, women themselves have often taken this perspective for granted. The postulate of objectivity in social science research has had schismatic effects on women, who—just like the copywriters with J. Walter Thompson—are taught to negate or ignore their experience as women in the pursuit of professional, academic excellence. This helps to explain why many women social scientists, even when studying women, have uncritically accepted analytic and theoretical constructs that "miss the deeper meaning" of the structural relationships between communications and the problem of gender (McCormack, 1983, pp. 281–82). Conversely, the declared pursuit of a woman-centered reevaluation of theories and methods has generally not served the "professional interests" of feminist scholars (Freeman, 1979; Evans, 1983; Stanley and Wise, 1983).

None of the "established" approaches to communication research has served women well. Even "critical" research, which "ideally addresses itself to the major issues of our time, and is concerned, amongst other things, with questioning the values and claims of the system, applying independent criteria, suggesting alternatives with regard to both means and ends, exploring the possibility of new forms and structures" (Halloran, pp. 168–69) has not—from a feminist perspective—lived up to its dazzling promise. It has, from this perspective, amounted to little more than "pouring new wine into old bottles" (Mies, 1983). It has not questioned the "basic assumptions, conventional wisdom, media myths, and the accepted ways of doing things" (Halloran, p.

171) embedded in and contributing to the structure of gender relationships. It offers no alternative, transformative visions of society. Women social scientists, however, taking their own sense of devaluation and struggle as a starting point, are a priori well equipped to contest the assumptions, myths, and accepted ways of doing things that bolster the androcentric structure of knowledge.

Jessie Bernard suggests that feminist scholars must go through a "major paradigm shift" to overcome the limitations imposed by a male-centered academic training. There is as yet no "adequate conceptual tool kit" for studying women's experience (Bernard, pp. 14-15). But this "double consciousness" of feminist social scientists (a realization of the contradictions in their own existence as women and as scholars) can also be interpreted as a methodological and political opportunity, rather than as an obstacle (Mies, pp. 120-21). Certainly, even if women have not yet developed the theoretical categories to express such contradictions, their pursuit demands new convergences and critical examination of traditional theories. Finally, such an approach has the potential to alter fundamentally the nature of *all* knowledge, information, and communication by shifting the focus from androcentricity to a frame of reference in which women's different and differing ideas, experiences, preoccupations, and interests are valid in their own right.

BIBLIOGRAPHIC REFERENCES

Arbeitsgruppe Frauenmaul. 1979. *Ich Hab' dir keinen Rosengarten Versprochen: Das Bild der Frau in vier Oesterreichischen Tageszeitungen—eine Dokumentation,* Vienna, Frischfleisch und Löwenmaul.

Baehr, Helen. 1980. "Out of Focus," *The Guardian,* London, May 6.

Bartos, Rena. 1982. *The Moving Target: What Every Marketer Should Know about Women,* New York, Free Press.

Bernard, Jessie. 1981. *The Female World,* New York, Free Press.

Black, Naomi, 1981. "The Future for Women and Development," in Black and Cottrell, eds., *Women,* pp. 265-85.

Black, Naomi, and Cottrell, Ann Baker, eds., *Women and World Change,* Beverly Hills, Calif., Sage Publ.

Bowles, Gloria, and Klein, Renate Duelli, eds., *Theories of Women's Studies,* London, Routledge and Kegan Paul.

Butler, Matilda, and Paisley, William. 1980. *Women and the Mass Media,* New York, Human Sciences Press.

Ceulemans, Mieke, and Fauconnier, Guido. 1979. *Mass Media: The Image, Role, and Social Condition of Women,* Paris, UNESCO (Reports and Papers on Mass Communication, no. 84).

Chabbra, Rami. 1980. "Women and the Media: What Strategies for Change?" Perspective paper for the UN/UNESCO Seminar on Women and the Media (May 20-23), New York.

Cuevas, Esmeralda Arboleda. 1980. *Influence of the Mass Communication Media on Attitudes towards the Roles of Women and Men in Present Day Society: Report to* the *UN Economic and Social Council,* New York, UN Economic and Social Council (E/CN 6/627/rev. 1).

Ehrenreich, Barbara, and Fuentes, Annette. 1981. "Life on the Global Assembly Line," *Ms. Magazine,* Jan.

Evans, Mary. 1983. "In Praise of Theory: The Case for Women's Studies," in Bowles and Klein, eds., *Theories,* pp. 219-28.

Ewen, Stuart. 1976. *Captains of Consciousness,* New York, McGraw-Hill.

Freeman, J. S. 1979. "The Feminist Scholar," *Quest,* vol. 5, no. 1, pp. 26-36.

Habib, Mariam. 1980. "Women and the Communications Workforce: A Profile of Lahore." Perspective paper for the UN/UNESCO Seminar on Women and the Media (May 20-23), New York.

Halloran, James D. 1982. "The Context of Mass Communication Research," in *Mass Communication Review Yearbook,* vol. 3, pp. 163-205.

Hanak, Katalin. 1982. "The Image of Women in the Radio," *Jel-Kep* (Journal of the Hungarian Mass Communication Research Center), special ed., Aug., pp. 97-127.

Heyzer, Noellen. 1982. "From Rural Subsistence to an Industrial Peripheral Work Force," in Lourdes Beneria, ed., *Women and Development: The Sexual Division of Labor in Rural Societies,* New York, Praeger, pp. 179-202.

Ide, Sachiko. 1978. "Language, Women, and the Mass Media in Japan," *Feminist Japan,* vol. 4, no. 1, pp. 22-24.

ISIS International Bulletin, 1982. Bulletin 24: *Women and New Technology.*

Jensen, Else. 1982. "Television Newscasts in a Women's Perspective." Paper presented at the 13th General Assembly and Conference of the International Association for Mass Communication Research, Paris, Sept. 6-10.

Karl, Marilee. 1981. "Alternative World Communication?" *ISIS International Bulletin,* 18:*Women and the Media,* pp. 26-29.

Kyaruzi, Agnes. 1975. "Women's Images in the Tanzanian Mass Media: Newspapers." Paper presented at the BRALUP (Bureau of Resource Assessment and Land Use Planning) Workshop on Women's Studies and Development, University of Dar es Salaam.

Gallagher, Margaret. 1979. *The Portrayal and Participation of Women in the Mass Media,* Paris, UNESCO (CC.79/WS/130).

———. 1980. *Images of Women in the Mass Media,* Paris, UNESCO (International Commission for the Study of Communication Problems, Doc. 59 bis).

———. 1981. *Unequal Opportunities: The Case of Women and the Media,* Paris, UNESCO Press.

———. 1984. "Employment and Positive Action for Women in Television in EEC Member States." Report on a project for the Commission of the European Communities.

Galtung, Johan. 1980. *The True Worlds: A Transnational Perspective,* New York, Free Press.

Glazer Schuster, Ilsa. 1979. *New Women of Lusaka,* Palo Alto, Cal., Mayfield.

Goonatilake, Hema. 1980. "Women in Creative Arts and Mass Media," in *Status of Women in Sri Lanka,* University of Colombo Press.

Leghorn, Lisa, and Parker, Katherine. 1981. *Woman's Worth: Sexual Economics and the World of Power,* Boston/London, Routledge and Kegan Paul.

Lebaube, Alain. 1984. "Germans Learn the Painful Lessons of Recession," *The Guardian Weekly,* London, July 1, p. 12.

Lim, Linda. 1980. "Women Workers in Multinational Corporations: The Case of the Electronics Industry in Malaysia and Singapore," in Krishna Kumar, ed., *Transna-*

tional Enterprises: Their Impact on Third World Societies and Cultures, Boulder, Colo., Westview, pp. 109-36.

MacBride, Seán, et al. 1980. *Many Voices, One World: Report by the International Commission for the Study of Communication Problems,* London/New York/Paris, Kogan Page/Unipub/UNESCO.

MacCormack, Thelma. 1980. "Machismo in Media Research," in *Mass Communication Review Yearbook,* vol. 1, pp. 574-85.

———. 1981. "Development with Equity for Women," in Black and Cottrell, eds., *Women,* pp. 15-30.

———. 1983. "Male Conceptions of Female Audiences: The Case of Soap Operas," in *Mass Communication Review Yearbook,* vol. 4, pp. 273-83.

McPhail, Thomas. 1981. *Electronic Colonialism,* Beverly Hills, Cal., Sage Publ.

Marzolf, Marion. 1977. *Up from the Footnote: A History of Women Journalists,* New York, Hastings House.

Mass Communication Review Yearbook. 1980. Vol. 1, G. Cleveland Wilhoit and Harold de Bock, eds., Beverly Hills, Cal., Sage Publ.

———. 1982. Vol. 3, D. Charles Whitney, Ellen Wartella, and Sven Windahl, eds.

———. 1983. Vol. 4, Ellen Wartella, D. Charles Whitney, and Sven Windahl, eds.

Mattelart, Michèle. 1981. *Les femmes et les industries culturelles,* Paris, UNESCO (Développement Culturel: Dossier Documentaire 23).

Media Report to Women. 1982. Vol. 10, nos. 11 and 12.

Meislin, Richard J. 1984. "Mexican Men Join Women's Preserve," *International Herald Tribune,* Paris, March 30, p. 11.

Mies, Maria. 1983. "Towards a Methodology for Feminist Research," in Bowles and Klein, eds., *Theories.*

Morgan, Robin. 1978. *Going too Far: The Personal Chronicle of a Feminist,* New York, Vintage.

Nuita, Yoko. 1979. *Impact of Audio Visual Media on Socio-Cultural Behavior of Women in Japan,* Paris, UNESCO (CC/CD/MED).

Pavlic, Breda, and Hamelink, Cees. 1982. *Interrelationship between the New International Economic Order and a New International/World Information Communication Order* (study prepared under contract to UNESCO), Ljubljana, Yugoslavia, Research Center for Cooperation with Developing Countries.

Pear, Robert. 1984. "Reagan's Policies Increased 'Poor,' Study Shows," *International Herald Tribune,* Paris, July 27, p. 3.

Robinson, Gertrude. 1978. "Women, Media Access, and Social Control," in Laurily Keir Epstein, ed., *Women and the News,* New York, Hastings House, pp. 87-108.

Rogers, Barbara. 1980. *The Domestication of Women: Discrimination in Developing Societies,* London, Tavistock.

Santa Cruz, Adriana, and Erazo, Vivian. 1980. *Cosmopolitan: El orden transnacional y su modelo femenino,* Mexico City, ILET (Instituto Latinoamericano de Estudios Transnacionales) and Editora Nueva Imagen.

Scott, Hilda. 1984. *The Feminisation of Poverty,* London, Pandora.

Siegel, Lenny. 1978. "Orchestrating Dependency," *Pacific Research,* vol. 9, nos. 5 and 6.

Stanley, Liz, and Wise, Sue. 1983. *Breaking Out: Feminist Consciousness and Feminist Research*, London, Routledge and Kegan Paul.

Tuchman, Gaye. 1978. *Making News: A Study in the Construction of Reality,* New York, Free Press.

United Nations. 1980. *The Economic Role of Women in the EEC Region,* New York (E. 80.II. E.6.).

United States Commission on Civil Rights. 1979. *Window Dressing on the Set: An Update,* Washington, D.C.

WCUNDW (World Conference on the UN Decade for Women). 1980a. *Program of Action for Second Half of the UN Decade for Women: Equality, Development, and Peace,* New York, United Nations (A/CONF. 94/34).

———. 1980b. *Review and Evaluation of Progress Achieved in the Implementation of the World Plan of Action: Political Participation, International Cooperation, and the Strengthening of International Peace,* New York, United Nations (A/CONF. 94/13).

———. 1980c. *Review and Evaluation. . . : Education,* New York, United Nations (A/CONF. 94/10).

———. 1980d. *Review and Evaluation. . . : Employment,* New York, United Nations (A/CONF. 94/8/rev. 1).

———. 1980e. *Review and Evaluation. . . : National Machinery and Legislation,* New York, United Nations (A/CONF. 94/11).

———. 1980f. *Information and Communication as Development Resources for the Advancement of Women,* New York, United Nations (A/CONF. 94/27).

———. 1980g. *Technological Change and Women Workers: The Development of Microelectronics,* New York, United Nations (A/CONF. 94/26).

Willetts, Peter, ed., *Pressure Groups in the Global System,* London, Frances Pinter.

Women Media Workers. 1978. *New Journalist* (special issue on the media presentation of women), Jan.

Working Party on Women in Broadcasting. 1981. *Report to the Radio Telefís Eireann Authority,* Dublin, Radio Telefís Eireann.

Worsley, Peter. 1984. *The Three Worlds: Culture and World Development,* London, Weidenfeld and Nicolson.

CHAPTER FOUR

African Responses to the NWICO Debate

Paul A. V. Ansah

One of the longest running and most controversial issues that has engaged the attention of the international community within the last decade is the debate on the New World Information and Communication Order (NWICO). The nature of the debate and the emotion, not to say acrimony, it has aroused is, in a sense, a recognition of the important role of mass communication in national affairs and in international relations. In developing countries, governments have become more aware of the role and potential of communication in development efforts and are committing greater resources to the provision of communication facilities. There is hardly any development plan that does not make greater investment in communication from one four- or five-year period to the next.

However, these increased investments in the provision of media facilities appear inadequate in relation to the needs of developing countries. Expanded facilities have augmented the resources enjoyed by urban elites at the expense of the disadvantaged rural poor, who have little access even to the most rudimentary modern media. This disparity at the national level is reflected in the gap between the availability of media resources and services in the industrialized countries of the North and the developing nations of the South at the international level.

This gap does not exist only in terms of physical facilities—newspapers, magazines, books, radio, television, telephone, telex, satellites, and computer facilities. It is much wider: developing countries are consumers of the communication products of the affluent industrialized countries, in terms of technical equipment and programs, especially in the electronic media. This increases the economic and cultural dependence of Third World countries and is at the core of the debate on a new world information and communication order.

For new nations having to address a whole new set of problems in their efforts at nation-building, an unregulated and unreciprocated flow of mass media products from developed countries can weaken the social fabric of their society and adversely affect their social, cultural, and even political values and thus pose a threat to their sovereignty. The objective of NWICO dialogue, therefore, is to seek a compromise solution that will ensure that international understanding is promoted through cultural contacts and a balanced flow of information, in place of the one-way flow that may result in what has been termed "cultural imperialism" or "cultural synchronization."[1]

Dialogue between North and South is expected to produce another result—namely, to help in redistribution of resources that will enable the countries of the South to communicate horizontally without necessarily having to pass through third parties, such as transnational news agencies. Though this dialogue has gone on for a long time, no spectacular results have yet been achieved. This is not said to deprecate the efforts that Third World countries, within the framework of the Non-Aligned Nations Movement, have made and continue to make to decrease their dependence on the industrialized nations, within the constraints of their limited resources. One recalls here the establishment of the Non-Aligned News Agencies Pool, the formation of the Union of African National Radio and Television (URTNA), and the setting up of the Pan-African News Agency (PANA), among other efforts.

The continuing debate on the establishment of a new world order in the field of information and communication has had one positive effect on the leaders of Africa and other developing areas: it has highlighted the various aspects of this multifaceted problem and heightened awareness of the need to formulate national communication policies that will respond to the needs of the various countries. The debate has thus been a form of education for national leaders and has obligated them to pay more attention to communication issues. In what follows here, I shall examine the efforts that African leaders have been making in this direction, the new orientations and structures needed to democratize communication, the personnel to be trained to administer communication apparatus, and other related issues.

I do not propose to examine all the various dimensions of NWICO; this paper will focus on the efforts being made in Africa to help achieve the objectives of NWICO, paying special attention to internal factors and situations that will accelerate or decelerate the process. For example, the question of technology that can create a situation of long-term dependence by the provision and servicing of equipment is a pertinent one in this discussion; however, I do not propose to deal with it, in view of my desire to concentrate on the structural dimensions and the use of human resources as they affect African perceptions of NWICO.

One important factor that has muddled NWICO dialogue and kept North and South apart (including in this case the East European socialist bloc) is the difference in perception of the role of the media in society and the relationship that exists between government and media. A rough distinction between the media system in the group of countries commonly referred to as Western democracies and that prevailing in Third World (and socialist) countries, the distinction drawn between a system based on free enterprise and a system based on state ownership and control. The African option for a state-controlled, service-oriented system is meant to respond to certain social, economic, political, and cultural factors, and it is perhaps necessary to throw some light on it before going further.

INFORMATION AND THE AFRICAN STATE

One striking fact about the media scene in Africa is the involvement of the state with information gathering, processing, and distributing. In many countries, the most important newspapers are owned by the state or the ruling political party. In some cases the state even holds a monopoly over the publishing of newspapers and magazines. This situation has resulted in abuses and has curtailed press freedom to such an extent that persons brought up in the Western libertarian tradition of the private ownership of newspapers tend to see state ownership as a sure index of lack of press freedom and a reflection of classic authoritarianism.

Although this is true in practice in a number of cases, a closer examination of the peculiar circumstances of Africa would seem to indicate that there is some justification for state involvement in the gathering, processing, and distribution of information through radio and the print media. State involvement with the electronic media is accepted in the vast majority of developed and developing countries throughout the world and provokes little controversy; it is state involvement with the print media that appears to be a departure from the traditions bequeathed to Africa and therefore provokes considerable controversy.

The media concept that appears to be followed in the vast majority of African countries is what W. A. Hachten has labeled the "developmental concept."[2] The rationale underlying this concept is that if the media are to be used to build national integration and mobilize the population for development, then the state should play a direct and active part in their functioning. Besides, governments feel that it is their direct responsibility to provide information to the people as a social service in the same way that they provide services in the areas of health, education, and recreation. It can therefore be argued that there is ideological justification for direct state operation of the mass media.

However, the exclusive or preponderant role of the state in the operation of newspapers often runs a course parallel with the establishment of one-party states, whether with a civilian or military government. The intolerance and rejection of ideological pluralism often displayed by such regimes seems to indicate that the "developmental concept" is often only a pretext for stifling all dissent within a state. If this were not so, one would see more mixed systems in which the state published newspapers side by side with privately owned ones, which would guarantee a diversity of information sources within the state. In most African countries, governments use either legislation or their economic power to discourage the emergence of privately owned newspapers. For example, by withholding import licences for the importation of equipment, newsprint, and other supplies, private entrepreneurs are prevented from venturing into the field of newspaper publication.

It should, however, be conceded that in some cases, even where governments have not discouraged private interests from going into the newspaper business, the general economic situation has not been favorable. In this context, it should be remembered that the tradition of the privately owned newspaper started in countries where there was a liberal, free market system that encouraged competition and gave rise to advertising, which provides the bulk of the income of a newspaper. This situation does not exist in Africa. Even in the few countries that have adopted the free market approach, economic activity is generally low, and there is a lack of variety in brands available, with the result that advertising does not provide enough revenue to support newspapers. Thus it is that political and economic factors combine to give the state a certain advantage in the production and distribution of information in Africa.

The point being made here is that state ownership of newspapers is not necessarily an indication of the lack of press freedom in an African country. That there is generally little press freedom is not in dispute, but the reasons for this situation have to be looked for elsewhere than in the question of ownership. In the case of news agencies, it is difficult to think of one that could exist in an African country as a private enterprise or cooperative. Most African countries have too few newspapers and usually a single radio station; their combined income would be hardly enough to pay the salaries of more than a handful of reporters. If governments did not run national news agencies, there would probably be no African country with a news agency.

It is only a deep appreciation of the peculiar circumstances in which the media have developed in Africa that will permit the creation of the proper atmosphere for coexistence and cooperation among states with different political and economic systems.

THE PAN-AFRICAN NEWS AGENCY (PANA)

Even before world attention came to be focused on the need for a New World Information and Communication Order (NWICO), Third World governments had recognized the need to "decolonialize" information. It was this concern that gave rise to the various consultations that culminated in the establishment of the Non-Aligned Countries News Agencies Pool. In the specific case of Africa, such efforts were started with the formation of the Organization of African Unity (OAU) in May 1963, but it was not until twenty years later that the Pan-African News Agency (PANA) started operations with a modest output of about 6,500 words a day, covering 25 stories. As of the end of 1983, this had been increased to between 15,000 and 17,000 words a day, covering 50 stories.

It is clear from the PANA Convention that it was established both as a political institution and as a mass media organization. As a political institution, PANA is enjoined in the Preamble of the Convention to "liberate African information from imperialist domination and foreign monopolies, and resolutely gear it towards the promotion of development." Further, Article 2a of the Convention assigns to PANA the role of promoting "the aims and objectives of the OAU for the consolidation of the independence, unity, and solidarity of Africa." As a mass media organization, PANA is enjoined on the professional level "to promote an effective exchange of political, economic, social, and cultural information among member states" (Art. 2c). It is an intergovernmental organization whose membership is made up not of national news agencies or other organs of information in the various countries, but of the member states of the OAU themselves.

Given the environment in which PANA was established, it is very easy to understand the emphasis on political objectives, but this very fact has some repercussions that may detract from the professional quality of its performance. For example, on the basis of the equality of all member states, PANA attempts to give equality of treatment to all member countries, and provided a state does not exceed its daily quota of 1,000 words, PANA is obliged to retransmit its reports, even if they are of little news value or poorly written. PANA has no editorial control over the material it receives and retransmits. PANA does, however, have some discretion in refusing to retransmit material that may be offensive to other countries or cause division among OAU members. This is a rather sensitive issue on which firm policies need to be formulated.

As a news agency pool, PANA has been operating as a kind of "post office" or retransmission center. If, as a result of the volume, a selection has to be made, it is done at one of the five regional centers, but once material is transmitted to PANA headquarters in Dakar, PANA has to retransmit without any editing: it has no gatekeeping or editorial control over news sent from a national source of information.

PANA can receive material directly from national sources or through its regional centers, of which there are five: Lagos for western Africa, Lusaka for southern Africa, Khartoum for eastern Africa, Kinshasa for central Africa, and Tripoli for northern Africa. Retransmission can also be made directly to those countries that have receiving facilities or through the regional centers.

In addition to serving as the center of a news agency pool, PANA can also act as a news agency in its own right, as it did when it covered the OAU summit conference in June 1983 in Addis Ababa, or the Fourteenth African Cup of Nations Football Competition in the Ivory Coast in March 1984. It can also transmit feature articles and special reports on developmental issues. It can detail its own correspondents to collect news from member states that have no national news agency, but only with their prior consent (Art. 6). As far as this aspect of its operations is concerned, PANA has full editorial control over the information it collects and produces by its own means. But PANA has very few reporters on its staff and cannot do this adequately. With the merger resources at its disposal and the inadequate telecommunication infrastructure in member states, PANA will do well to concentrate more on features with a developmental content than on spot news that quickly becomes outdated.[3]

After less than one year of operation, it is difficult to measure the impact of PANA on the flow of news among member countries. However, it is noteworthy that by the end of the first six months of its operation, over thirty national news agencies were sending material to PANA and receiving material from it, with ten of them doing so on a daily basis. In terms of the use of PANA material, it is still more difficult to estimate the impact because many African newspapers and broadcasting stations hardly ever credit their sources. However, an examination of a two-month output of stories from PANA to a typical African news agency leaves one in little doubt about the very small percentage of material that is used. This is because sometimes dispatches have little news value beyond the national frontiers of the originating countries; in other cases, the material is so poorly written that if PANA had editorial control, it would edit it before retransmission.

In order to improve the quality of reporting, PANA held two meetings, one in August 1983 in Dakar and the other in October in Lusaka for editors-in-chief of African national news agencies. The meetings treated of the PANA stylebook, standards to be maintained, and the training of staff. As a result of these and other planned meetings, it is hoped that a fairly uniform view of which national stories will interest readers in other parts of Africa and how to write in conformity with the PANA stylebook will emerge.

But even when these problems have been solved, PANA has a few other problems to contend with before it can make the impact desired of it. The most formidable of these problems is that of finance; some member states are unable to pay their contributions on time and this makes it difficult for the agency to acquire equipment or hire personnel. One category of personnel whose recruitment is particularly urgent is that of translators. At the moment, PANA operates in the three official languages of the OAU—Arabic, English, and French. It retransmits material in the language of reception, so that material originating from French-speaking news agencies is transmitted in French to English-speaking news agencies. Inasmuch as national news agencies have no translators of their own, such stories are not used—which is a great waste of resources. If PANA had its own translators, such material could first be translated before retransmission. This would cause some delay, but at least the material would arrive in a language understood by recipients and could then be evaluated and used if found newsworthy or suitable. It would certainly make better sense for PANA to have translators at headquarters than to expect individual national news agencies to have translators or bilingual reporters on their staffs.

One other problem being faced by PANA, and which may account for its stories not being used much, is that, as a result of delays occasioned by transmission first to Dakar and thence to regional centers for retransmission or directly to national news agencies, deadlines are not met: material arrives late. Besides, some states do not have the appropriate equipment for receiving PANA material. This situation is further compounded by the fact that apart from Lusaka and Khartoum, the regional centers from which stories should be relayed to national agencies were not operating as of the end of 1983. For all these reasons, it is difficult and premature to assess the impact that the establishment of PANA has made on the flow of news among the nations of the continent.

But if PANA is to make any impact on the flow of news among the nations of Africa, it is essential that it establish a reputation for credibility. One fear expressed by some African editors, though in hushed tones, is that because of the excessive government control over the media in certain countries, there is a reasonable suspicion that the national news agencies that feed into PANA may only be propaganda organs of their governments and not objective, fair, and dependable sources of information. The heavy political tone of the PANA Convention can only lend weight to such suspicions.

NWICO AND COMMUNITY MEDIA

In the debate on NWICO, considerable attention has been paid to the international dimensions of the problem, but national and local issues have not been given the emphasis they merit. Though disparities in communication facilities exist in all parts of the world, they are much more glaring in the countries of the Third World, particularly in Africa. The largest newspapers and magazines are published in capitals or large regional centers and most of their readers live in urban areas. Television in Africa is an urban phenomenon, and though radio can be considered the only truly mass medium with deep penetration into rural areas, minority language groups do not get as much out of radio as those who speak the official language or a major national language.

In terms of content too, newspapers tend to be urban-oriented, paying scant attention to rural affairs. Those who generate news and occupy the front pages of the newspapers are political leaders, government officials, and other persons belonging to the upper and middle social classes. Radio attempts to cater to the needs of the illiterate rural majority, but even here, because of centralized broadcasting systems and the multiplicity of languages, individual language groups get little out of radio that is relevant to their concerns.

What this means in practical terms is that rural dwellers in general, and linguistic and cultural minorities in particular, are not given the opportunity to participate fully in national life. They do not have adequate facilities for being informed or for voicing their feelings and participating, even if only indirectly, in the taking of decisions that affect their lives. If rural dwellers are deprived in terms of sheer physical facilites for communication through the mass media, deprivation is even greater when it comes to participation in the production of programs. Rural dwellers are generally treated—and this applies to urban populations too—as passive recipients of information selected, processed, and packaged for them by professionals.

In order to reduce disparities within countries and ensure a certain amount of access and participation by a larger section of the population, the most obvious solution would be to decentralize the media system so that individual, localized newspapers and radio stations could concern themselves with problems originating from the localities within which they operate. The decentralization of radio would give more broadcast time to specific language groups and put more emphasis on programs that are of greater relevance to local populations, bringing communication nearer to democratization. Decentralization would also help to discover and develop the talents and creative gifts of local populations.

In Africa, the need for the democratization of communication through decentralization is not particularly well appreciated. It is argued that communication facilities should be used to forge a sense of national unity and integration by creating national symbols and creating national loyalty in place of ethnic loyalties. The decentralization of communication is therefore seen as a threat to the ideal of creating national cohesion; a decentralized system is thought to contain the potential for divisiveness in this period of nation-building. However, a few attempts are being made, the most publicized one being the Homa Bay radio experiment in Kenya. The success or failure of that experiment will determine the prospects for decentralized broadcasting systems and community radio stations in Africa.[4]

In the case of the print media, over fifty rural or community newspapers were set up in sixteen subsaharan African countries since 1971, mainly on the initiative and encouragement of UNESCO. The vast majority are published in the local languages for the benefit of the newly literate in rural areas. These rural or community papers are conceived both as sources of information and as development tools. Because of their limited circulation, printing costs are high and there is hardly any advertising revenue to offset costs. Most of these papers are facing financial and personnel problems, but evaluation studies done on selected papers indicate that they have a great potential for stimulating literacy and social development and for helping to integrate rural dwellers into national life.

It would seem that African leaders do not appear to be aware of the great potential that the rural newspaper has for democratizing communication. They appear unwilling to commit needed resources to the establishment of more rural or community newspapers and the expansion of existing ones. In many cases, these papers were established on an experimental basis on the initiative of UNESCO, and when UNESCO decided to pull out at the end of the experimental period, it meant the virtual drying up of all financial assistance and the beginning of the battle for survival.

NWICO AND THE TRAINING OF MEDIA PERSONNEL

For a fuller appreciation of the New World Information and Communication Order, it is important to view it at the international and national levels. NWICO calls at once for the decolonization of information at the international level and the democratization of communication at the national level. Its ultimate objective is to promote international understanding and intranational harmony. This way of looking at NWICO has certain implications for training and curriculum development in the field of communication studies.

It must be noted that the call for a New World Information and Communication Order was initiated and articulated by the nonaligned nations as a further step in the movement toward decolonization and the reduction of dependency. It was seen as another perspective in the fight to end the situation of political, economic, and cultural dependency. In order, therefore, that communication students appreciate the full import of NWICO, it is essential that their curriculum deal with the structures of the international economic systems that have, to a certain extent, determined the perception of what constitutes information and the directions in which it flows. This will clearly bring out the organic relationship between the New World Economic Order and the New World Information and Communication Order.

It is also essential that the different media systems and their underpinning philosophies be critically examined in relation to the function and role of the media in various societies so that inappropriate models are not followed. It is implied in this recommendation that basic training, certainly at the undergraduate level, should be provided locally in a familiar environment so that trainees are in direct contact with the cultural context, traditions, value systems, development needs, and environmental priorities in which they will later be working. A further implication is that there should be less dependence on foreign models, though students should be made aware of them for purposes of comparison.

As far as meeting national needs is concerned, the training of media personnel should aim at producing specialists to work in areas of social and economic development. This means that training should aim not only at equipping trainees with skills to produce material for information, broad education, and entertainment, but also at equipping them with techniques for using communication in a purposeful and persuasive way. It can be said that traditional training in communication aims at teaching trainees to preserve the status quo; the new orientation in training should be geared toward persons who will try to change and transform society. For example, students should be trained to get away from the event-oriented spot news approach and learn how to analyze and describe social processes.

The kind of training that one comes across in the traditional, vocation-oriented training institution equips trainees to serve a majority of urban elite that is literate and can afford the latest electronic media gadgets. But social justice demands that the interests of the disadvantaged, illiterate, rural poor, who form the majority, should also be provided for. This can best be accomplished through the training of media personnel in the use of minimedia—community radio and the rural or community newspaper in which a local population participates both as producer and consumer of program content. In this context, the training of media personnel should aim at the eventual evolution of a participatory communication system that will ultimately replace the existent vertical and hierarchical system.

Realization of the need to bridge the communication gap between rural and urban populations, as well as recognition of the important role that communication can play in development, have prompted a few mass communication training institutions in Africa, especially those that are university-based, to try to put together programs designed to offer more than traditional courses in the training of journalists and broadcasters. Traditional courses in print and broadcast journalism are offered, but in addition there are a number of courses related to developed issues as well as to the social and economic problems of Africa. The objective of the university-based courses is thus to train communicators in the broader sense, rather than journalists or broadcasters in the narrower sense. These training courses are based on the assumption that in order to respond to the needs of Africa, communicators need a broader background, one that can transform them into agents for social change.

This same sentiment was expressed at a UNESCO seminar on media training held in Kuala Lumpur in June 1973. It was emphasized that a background in liberal and social studies was necessary for the training of media personnel:

> If the media are to be socially constructive, they must be based on intelligent understanding of the social, cultural, and economic issues which they report. This can come about only if the people who speak and write are themselves intelligently informed.[5]

The seminar went on to recommend that, for the needs of a developing country, a certain amount of specialization in such areas as education, health, nutrition, family planning, agriculture, economics, management, public relations, and advertising might be in order after the basic skills had been acquired.

This concept of communication training marks a considerable advance over the kind offered in the traditional, vocation-oriented training institutions. These traditional institutions pay scant or no attention at all to communication theory or to studies in interpersonal or small-group communication, which are very useful in promoting development, whether these particular techniques are used alone or in combination with the mass media, as in the case of radio forums.

Furthermore, there is the question of how to reach the great numbers of those who cannot read the official languages—French or English—or even their own languages, but who need to be brought into the development process through meaningful communication. This means, for example, exploring the use that can be made of traditional communication and art forms, popular media and folk culture, which have a potential for constituting effective channels of interpersonal communication in the design and transmission of material that will lead to the adoption of innovative attitudes and practices.

Even though the need for a new orientation in communication training has been recognized in Africa, training institutions do not appear to be moving fast enough in putting the necessary changes into effect. Even though communication training institutions have grown in number on the continent within the last two decades, with a few offering courses at the undergraduate and graduate levels, it is doubtful whether the quantitative increase has also meant a qualitative increase in the formulation of appropriate courses suitable for the specific needs of developing countries.

The major factor impeding the desired development is that of staff personnel. Many of the instructors who should initiate moves in the new direction have been trained in Europe or North America, where teaching programs are generally not adapted to the needs of developing countries. It requires considerable effort to abandon familiar models in favor of new ones, and the necessary effort is not always made.

Another factor is the relative paucity of appropriate teaching materials. Most of the textbooks used are based on the experiences of developed countries. However, within the last two decades, considerable literature on development and communication models based on the experiences of other Third World countries in Asia and Latin America with fairly similar experiences has been developed and can be more easily adapted to the needs of Africa. The availability of this material does not, however, discharge African communication scholars from the responsibility of producing appropriate and relevant teaching materials themselves.

The need to reorientate African communication trainers themselves to develop teaching materials and make their courses more relevant to the needs of the continent has been recognized by the African Council on Communication Education (ACCE). In 1983 and 1984 it organized workshops on the sociology of communication and communication for rural development. The objective of both workshops was to sensitize instructors to the need for changing the direction of training to make it more relevant to the needs of Africa within the context of development and NWICO.

CONCLUSIONS

It is clear from what has been said above that the debate on NWICO stimulated fresh thinking in Africa on the role of communication in nation-building. Even though there had been an awareness of the pertinent issues before the NWICO debate started, discussions have accelerated the efforts being made by individual African countries to find solutions to the problems involved. There has also been a move from the debate level to the action level.

In this context, the most significant action has been the establishment of PANA.

Although PANA is facing a number of teething problems, its very establishment and the fact that more member countries are contributing to it by sending material indicate the importance that Africans attach to the agency, but a lot more still needs to be done. PANA needs more injection of funds to put its operations on a sounder footing. It also needs the support of PANAFTEL and PATU to obtain the necessary telecommunication infrastructure to speed up the transmission and reception of material. But above all, it may be necessary at an early stage to review the PANA Convention with a view to softening its political overtones and giving it a more professional outlook. This is the only way in which it can establish a record of credibility and reliability, so that PANA material could be useful not only to Africans but to users outside Africa as well.

In the field of training, a number of institutions were established before the NWICO debate became topical. However, the debate has generated some further thinking about the objectives of media training in an African context and some of these institutions are responding to the challenges. For this reason, there is a departure from the traditional vocational training to a more interdisciplinary approach. However, a lot more changes need to be effected in the various curricula to adequately prepare trainees for the environment in which they will work after their training.

It has been said that the NWICO debate can be summarized in four D's: decolonization, democratization, demonopolization, and development.[6] The first two Ds deal specifically with the international dimensions of NWICO. In the area of development and democratization, we have seen some feeble efforts being made to bring the media closer to the people through community radio and rural or community newspapers. However, this approach implies the decentralization of the media system, which has certain political implications and cannot be easily overlooked. It also requires greater financial investments, which the fragile economies of African countries cannot provide, particularly in a period of depression. It is hoped that when the economic situation improves, the few experiments in community media taking place in certain African countries will produce results that will encourage others to give greater access to their people both in the production and the consumption of media programs relevant to their concerns and expressive of their cultural values.

But above all, it should be remembered that whatever comes out of the NWICO debate, not much will have been achieved as long as the vast majority of Africans are denied freedom of expression and access to information in their own countries. In the area of free self-expression, the African record is not a particularly brilliant one. Freedom of expression and other rights have been denied Africans in the name of accelerated national development. The evidence shows clearly that the most authoritarian and repressive regimes are by no means the most developed ones. And this very fact should provoke some new thinking on the internal media systems of African countries.

NOTES

1. "Cultural synchronization" is a term that Cees J. Hamelink uses in his book, *Cultural Autonomy and Global Communication* (New York, Longman, 1983). The author explains his preference for this new term: "In the international literature, this phenomenon is usually described as cultural imperialism. I give preference to the concept of cultural synchronization, which is more precise for my purposes. In my view, cultural imperialism is the most frequent but not exclusive, form in which cultural synchronization occurs. Cultural synchronization can take place without imperialistic relations constituting the prime causal factor or even without any overt imperialistic relations" (p. 5).

2. Hachten (*The World News Prism,* Iowa State University Press, 1981) reviews the traditional classification of the world media system and comes up with his own five distinguishing concepts of the press as: authoritarian, Western, communist, revolutionary, or developmental. Countries that adopt the developmental concept are described in the book as "nonindustrialized non-Communist nations of the Third World" (pp. 60-77).

3. Most of my factual information on PANA was obtained from a paper presented at a workshop on NWICO by Mr. D. K. Afreh, administrative deputy director-general of PANA. The workshop was sponsored by the African Council on Communication Education (ACCE) in Nairobi, Oct. 8–16, 1983. Interpretations of the data and conclusions drawn from them are my own.

4. For a fuller discussion of this issue, using Ghana as an example, see P. A. V. Ansah: "Problems of Localizing Radio in Ghana," *Gazette,* vol. 25, no. 4, 1979, pp. 1–16.

5. UNESCO: *Training for Mass Communication,* Reports and Papers on Mass Communication, no. 73, 1975, p. 17.

6. Kaarle Nordenstreng, "Defining the New International Information Order," in *World Communication—A Handbook*, George Gerbner and Marsha Siefert, eds., New York and London, Longman, 1983, p. 34.

CHAPTER FIVE

NWICO: New World Information and Communication Order

Washington Uranga

INTRODUCTION

During the preparatory stages for the third general conference of the Latin American episcopate (Puebla, Mexico, 1979), the bishops of the Department of Social Communication of CELAM (the Latin American Episcopal Council) drafted a document that, in my opinion and that of many others working in the sphere of communications in Latin America, is one of the most valuable contributions of the church on the subject of communication and its relation to social reality. Its greatest value is not so much in the novelty of the theoretical statements put forward, as in the fact that the preparatory work for Puebla gathered together the experience of many years of pastoral presence by the Latin American church in the field of communication.

In that document, "Evangelization and Social Communication in Latin America,"[1] Latin American bishops maintain that "social communication must be at the service of social change and human development,"[2] insisting that communication must "collaborate in the creation of a plan for liberation

---

This paper was first presented to the OCIC/UNDA conference, "Communication and Human Development: Challenges for Today," Nairobi, Kenya, November 26-29, 1983.

capable of securing peaceful, fair, and friendly conditions for our peoples."[3]

History is understood as an indivisible whole and communication as one facet that must necessarily be considered in its historical context. That vision was later ratified and adopted in Puebla, when it was said that "social communication is conditioned by the socio-cultural reality of our countries. It, in turn, is one of the determining factors in maintaining that reality" (Puebla, no. 1067).[4]

"Evangelization, the proclamation of the Kingdom, is communication" (Puebla, no. 1063). The first statement from the Latin American bishops in Puebla specifically referring to communication completes our terms of reference. And it is all in perfect harmony with the vision put forward by Paul VI, that human development, liberation, and evangelization are not realities that can be divided or separated, but merely diverse aspects of the building of the same history that leads us to the kingdom of God.[5]

Our mission as Christians demands from us an active presence in history. "Our social conduct is an integral part of our following of Christ" (Puebla, no. 476). "Evangelization would not be complete if it did not take account of the unceasing interplay of the Gospel and of man's concrete life, both personal and social" (*Evangelii Nuntiandi,* no. 35).

Our responsibility as conscientious communicators of the reality of misery and injustice faced by contemporary peoples, especially those in Latin America and other parts of the Third World, confronts us with the challenge, expressed by Pope John Paul II in his message to the World Meeting for Social Communications of 1983, to place communication at the disposal of peace, the building of justice, the encouragement of democratic participation between persons and peoples.

This is the fundamental starting point of the reflections that follow: a study of the problem from the perspective of the church, the course the church has followed in this respect throughout the years, and our responsibility as Christian communicators.

The challenges spring from our own Christian vocation, from the painful reality outlined by human history and also from the responses that individuals themselves make, not without great difficulty, and to which both Christians and the church must pay special attention.

These reflections on communication and human development seek to highlight those elements in Latin American reality and experience that, in the context of the New International Economic Order (NIEO) and the New World Information and Communication Order (NWICO) will help to overcome the present situation. These same elements challenge the church and demand its attention.

UNDERSTANDING THE PROBLEM OF COMMUNICATION TODAY

Communication is at the very heart of social experience. The MacBride Report—the reflections of experts commissioned by UNESCO to consider the problem of communication on a worldwide basis—states that communication "maintains and animates life," is an "expression on social activity and civilization," and a "common pool of ideas" (MacBride Report, p. 19).[6]

Nevertheless, despite the fact that social practice daily indicates the contrary, there is continual insistence on equating "communication" with "the media." This is an erroneous oversimplification frequently made not only by church representatives but also by media professionals, reducing the reality of communication to its merely instrumental aspect. This misunderstanding gives rise to misleading analysis—the source, in turn, of erroneous policies and procedures.

Despite the seriousness of this error from both the theoretical and practical points of view, there is no need for me to disprove it here: its falsity is very evident. But it would be wrong to suppose that, because this reductionist view has been overcome at the theoretical level among media specialists, it has also lost the support of those who, without being theoreticians or specialists, have particular responsibilities in communication, from origination and production to the formulation of policies.

The problem exists, both inside and outside the church, and we should bear it in mind even if it is not dealt with here.

Communication as a Global Phenomenon

According to the Puebla Final Document:

The term "culture" means the specific way in which human beings belonging to a given people cultivate their relationship with nature, with each other, and with God. . . . So conceived, culture embraces the whole life of a people. It is the whole web of values that inspire them and of disvalues that debilitate them; insofar as they are shared by all the members, they bring them together on the basis of a "collective consciousness" [Puebla, nos. 386-87].

In their relationships with nature, human beings try to master and transform it. With their peers and with God they create networks of social and religious relationships, searching continuously to learn from their experience (historical memory), in order to plan the future (historical self-projection). Culture is a historical and social reality in constant transformation (cf. Puebla, no. 392). All its aspects are connected at the level of the same fulfilling experience of the person, its relationships governed by common rules, norms, and values, creating the "collective consciousness" referred to by Puebla—in other words, making possible the creation of a cultural context within which all actions, initiatives, relationships, manifestations, and aspirations are ruled by the same code. Therefore, correct understanding and interpretation of these actions, initiatives, and aspirations will be possible only within the same cultural context, where each of them has meaning and finds adequate interpretation. Outside this cultural context, understanding will fail.

Communication, "a continual exchange between equals, or at least between reciprocally responsible partners," is at the very basis of cultural reality (MacBride Report, p. 149). By constantly relating persons to one another, it becomes itself a social relationship creative of culture—that is to say, it generates common values, norms, and rules of behavior that become a part of the collective consciousness. Communication facilitates cultural synthesis: it allows for the socialization of the elements that constitute the cultural context.[7] Communication interacts with the social, political, and economic levels of society as a whole, within the ideologico-institutional framework imposed by the groups that set the pace in each society. Within this framework, culture and communication become the fundamental arena for the contest between social sectors trying to gain positions in society. Control of communication, implementation of a given policy of communication, can become a major factor for or against a given social undertaking.

At least two immediate consequences derive from these premises. First it is impossible to analyze communication in isolation. Any analysis must be closely related to the social factors that condition and determine it and upon which communication simultaneously exerts its own influence. The object of analysis is society and its members. Communication is but one of the elements to be considered. Only within the socio-historical framework can a particular analysis of communication be undertaken. And it will be valid only if it takes into account the total framework, including economic, socio-political, and cultural realities and the information that comes from transformative human action on these realities.

Secondly, it is not possible to plan communication work in isolation from general social practice, which must be disposed to the social self-projection envisaged by planners. Any attempt to change the reality of communication must be supported by an intrasocietal project that serves as a framework for redefinitions in this specific field and defines this work within the overall task of social change.

To demand that analysis of communication and social practices seeking the transformation of the present system of communications should relate to global standards, and to a social project in which communication is contained and its function socially determined, entails not only a problem of method. It entails the reaffirmation of a common history where all structural levels and social groups are dialectically related in a kind of interaction that produces qualitative differences.

At a very concrete level, this understanding avoids a simplistic approach that would either place responsibility for all the problems of society on the media or absolve them of all social responsibility, the implication being that they act as an independent wheel in the social machine.

On the other hand, this global vision destroys the illusion, entertained by some, that by using the resources of communication in a technically and methodically appropriate manner, marvelous changes take place, almost magically, to modify any level of social reality.

Both mistakes, very frequent in certain church circles, prompt faulty diagnosis and faulty practice, which bring as a consequence ineffectiveness for the work planned and frustration for those doing the work. In both cases technology is then saddled with a culpability or responsibility that rightfully belongs to the social practices of human beings.

In short, communication work cannot be separated from social practice and the task of evangelization. Social utopia and the kingdom of God are the conceptual frameworks that give meaning to communication. Communication tasks are analyzed, criticized, and elaborated in relation to them, as an integral part of the same plan to establish more just social relationships, in the process of liberation that works toward building the kingdom of God.

The task of communication in a Third World slum area, urban or rural, must of necessity start with the living conditions of the people, the problems and aspirations of the people. Communication, as a social and technological reality, cannot take place in isolation, and has to contribute to the consolidation of a historical plan for better conditions, and a model of society that ensures a just, egalitarian, and comradely way of life.

Similarly, the proclamation of the gospel, even if it is made through the best resources provided by the technology of communication, will not find fertile soil if the message is foreign to the social reality and culture of the particular community.

Transnationalization and World Crisis

The global perspective referred to above obliges me to investigate, at least briefly, some aspects of the kind of analysis that will permit correct assessment of the problem of communication. The analysis of communication demands an in-depth study of social, economic, political, and cultural problems. To do otherwise would mean making the same mistake already mentioned. I shall list here only the general aspects of such an analysis.

We live in a world that revolves around a small number of centers of transnational power, characterized by a concentration of economic and political power that uses culture as a means of penetrating and domesticating the peripheral sectors subject to domination by the center.

The transnationalization of the economy and of political power overcame the old bipolarity between the socialist and the capitalist blocs represented in the postwar period by the Soviet Union and the United States of America. It is impossible to state today with certainty that the governments of these countries continue to be centers of transnational power, although their interests coincide to a great extent with the interest of the transnational centers of power. What is most clearly perceptible at present is a multilateral and transnational world, with suprastate interests at the economic and political levels, and more than ever before at the financial level.

We live in a world in which interdependence is not equally balanced, in which the organization of production, the use of resources, and the policies applied to them are planned according to the interests of transnational corporations. National boundaries have been overstepped.

It is in the clash of interests of these transnational groups that the real reasons and motives behind the problems that affect the modern world should be sought. It is an oversimplification to return again and again to accusations against one or another state, pointing it out as the only culprit. This must be kept in mind in analyzing the reality of countries both in the West and the East, in Latin America or any other part of the Third World.

So, for example, it is not possible to see the conflict between Great Britain and Argentina over the Falkland Islands in the South Atlantic simply as a territorial dispute between two nations. Behind it lay an economic-military potential in which the transnational industrial-military apparatus was interested. And there was a direct correlation between control of the South Atlantic, its possibilities for communications, and Antarctic resources.

If this were not the case, it would not be possible to understand why the superpowers, which continually confront each other with military, verbal, and diplomatic attacks, are in agreement when it comes to imposing the same conditions of unfavorable exchange on poor countries—conditions generally fixed by transnational oligopolies that control the market of all basic products.

The battle is for markets, financial interests, and basic raw materials. In this battle, technology has become the means to bedazzle and attract the countries on the periphery, as did European conquerors in the Americas, offering necklaces, mirrors, and trinkets in exchange for the hospitality and wealth of indigenous peoples.

Culture is but another battlefield, where transnational powers attempt to widen their area of domination over peripheral zones.

But confirming the existence of transnational centers of world power does not absolve local communities of responsibility. In each country there are national social sectors established as centers of power within juridical, institutional, and economic structures that act as allies and accomplices of transnational interests in exchange for economic benefits and participation in the sharing of power. These sectors, nominally national and belonging to a certain stratum of the social and juridical-institutional structure, are in charge of carrying out the policies dictated by the centers of transnational power, thus obviating the need for direct intervention by power centers represented by dominant states or nations.

Even among peoples suffering under the worst conditions of domination and deprivation, examples can be found of attitudes that, far from supporting the growth of collective consciousness in favor of liberation, go against the interests of the worst off and favor transnational domination.

The transnational understanding of world reality does not contradict the theory of the international division of labor. On the contrary, it supports the existence of central zones, where high levels of industrial and technological development occur at the cost of other areas in the world, marginal and peripheral, which act as suppliers of raw materials to and markets for products from the industrialized world. To verify this statement it is only necessary to realize that a large number of Third World countries have not succeeded in developing even the minimal infrastructures that would allow them to extend the process of eliminating the need to import light industrial products.

There is where the Third World stands: a marginal zone to the transnational central powers, a producer of raw materials, and a potential market for the industrial products of the center.

To the above must be added one other factor, of a conjunctural nature: the world crisis affecting the whole of humankind. To define this crisis a group of experts meeting in Embú, Brazil, in 1982, pointed out the following in their statement entitled "The Church and NWICO":

> The economic crisis that affects the whole world highlights the injustices and incongruencies of the economic systems that determine relationships between countries. In Latin America, the interest of the ruling elites, supported by unjust structures, aggravate the effects of the crisis. These injustices, which are the result of lengthy historical processes, become unbearable in the present crisis, for they deeply affect the balance of the world economy. *It is no longer a question of internal consequences for this or that country, for the socialist or the capitalist bloc, but of risks that affect everyone.* There lies the root of the problem, whose treatment should be based on the universality of human interests rather than on financial or technological difficulties [Embú, nos. 5-7; emphasis added].[8]

It is the context of the transnationalization of all social relationships and of world crisis that our situation relative to culture and communication should be understood. To move away from this framework and to ignore it when explaining reality is a grave misjudgment. It leads to fallacious analysis and inadequate attempts to rectify the situation. Realities as complex as those of radio, cinema, and television must be studied in direct relation to this perception of wholeness and within the context of a "culture industry" that has also been transnationalized.

The Culture Industry

I understand "culture industry" to be the system of producing and distributing symbolic goods—comparable with any other type of industrial production.

From the economic point of view, the culture industry, which includes the communication industry, is based on a heavy concentration of economic power due to the large investment it demands, and a large market that consumes its products and justifies the investments made. As a result, there is an inevitable subordination of work and cultural production to the economic interests of capital. Some immediate consequences of this fact are, among others, the concentration of the power of decision over cultural production in the hands of persons or centers of power linked to capital and not to culture; the manipulation of language in order to serve predetermined consumption trends; imposition of a very rapid rhythm of production that prioritizes the need for quantity and ignores any demand for quality. Because of a factor inherent in capitalist industry, any product, even culture, is highly perishable—which fosters continual use and reuse of the industrial process.

Consider how quickly a song or a record is put on the market, with all the help of the mass media, until the desired sales target is reached. Once this has been achieved, another cultural offering will replace the first one, rapidly creating a new need that will at the same time dampen the appeal of the previous "hit," rendering it obsolete.

Another consequence of the culture industry is "transculturalization." In the careful language of the MacBride Report, it is acknowledged that the culture industry "can create a cultural environment affected by undesirable external influences, or marked by uniformity and stereotyping" (p. 99).

But relationships between culture industry and capital are not limited to the economic sphere; they can also be seen at the ideological level. The culture industry, through the mass media, acts as a vehicle for penetration and ideological subordination of peripheral zones with a view to incorporating them in the ideologico-cultural framework of the ruling sectors.

The "message" confronts the consumer in the South with the media image of reality in the North presented as the only true reality. The values of "successful" groups in contemporary society are glorified and held forth as the model to aim at, worthy of imitation. Fragments of reality are presented as if they were all that exist. What gives immediate results, as opposed to the quest for more profound causes, is extolled.

It is urgent that we denounce the flood of television advertisements coming from the U.S.A. and reflecting cultural values totally foreign to the lifestyles of our peoples. No less serious is the fact that, as an expression of colonial mentality, even Latin American media productions often replicate, with our own landscapes and national characteristics, the cultural patterns and aspirations of North American productions.

It is possible to identify three basic characteristics in most of the cultural products that originate in transnational industry and alienate Third World consumers:

a) The presentation of a cultural reality foreign to that of viewers seeking to identify with it, and the total underestimation and disregard for viewer's own cultural values.

b) Fragmentation and division of reality, ignoring the global view and the context of facts. The "here and now" is the "truth," allowing no room for a broader global understanding of reality.

c) The yen for immediate results invalidates the search for the deeper meaning, the raison d'etre, of events, and their place within a scheme of development suited to cultural patterns. Consumers find themselves compelled toward the frequently and urgently reiterated choice of foregoing in-depth analysis if they do not want to "forfeit the present opportunity."

Within the problem of cultural invasion, advertising has special importance. Usually it is the privileged bearer of the prevailing ideology; it is closely related to the centers of economic domination. Advertising is one of the fundamental props of a consumer society.

Cultural Invasion

The development of the culture industry has taken the form of "invasion" or "cultural penetration" of peripheral countries. Paulo Freire, quoted by Heriberto Muraro in his work on cultural invasion in Latin America, describes it in the following terms:

> Cultural invasion is action in the field of culture that serves the aims of conquest and continues oppression; it implies a narrow view of reality, a static perception of facts and the imposition on others of a certain conception of the world. It implies the "superiority" of the invader and the "inferiority" of the invaded, and the imposition of values [Muraro, *La invasión*].[9]

The mere choice of the term "cultural invasion" to describe this type of aggression constitutes in itself an implicit stand, a task of denunciation marked out by researchers in communication, according to Muraro in the work mentioned above. To call the phenomenon "invasion" is to assign it the character of aggression and take the first steps toward self-defense.

It is useful, in trying to understand this problem, to describe some of the characteristics that are usually present in the process of cultural invasion. In general, the elements presented here can be applied to all the countries in the Third World, although it is logical to suppose that there are cases that deserve special study, especially in countries where fundamental social and political changes have recently taken place.

More than simply penetrating, the mass media graft themselves onto the realities of peripheral countries. The attack takes place with impressive speed—all the speed needed to establish, disseminate, and expand the media in poor countries. In Latin America the rapid spread of television reinforced this effect. Television "made visible," in a way unknown at least to the popular sectors, the image of a "successful" culture. Television "materialized" the values of the invading culture that until then had remained "abstract."

In the period after the Second World War, acceleration in technological developments not only increased the efficiency of the task imposed by the center but also stimulated the need for capital to look for new markets that would help make a return on investments. This also stimulated a new kind of presence by transnational corporations: investment in the communications industry (radio broadcasting, television enterprises, advertising agencies, etc.) in peripheral countries. This new kind of presence was well received in poor countries, eager to put into practice a development model that would take them rapidly toward the elimination of dependence on imports.

This whole process was made easier by the weak ideological structure of the ruling sectors of the poor countries, demonstrated by their incapacity and passivity in establishing national policies that would counteract the transnationals. On the contrary, the massive presence of transnational corporations, their establishment in local markets, and the effects of modernization that they produce in the structures of communication are appreciated in most cases (and here the concrete example of cultural alienation mentioned earlier can be seen) as a sign of development, their real but limited scope not taken into account.

However, cultural invasion does not always have the effect expected by the ruling classes. Although some sectors within the national oligarchies represent transnational interests, there are also contradictions between the national bourgeoisie and the interests of the transnational corporations. Such contradictions must be studied in each specific case, based on the changing social situation of each country. But the truth is that these contradictions have become, at the economic level, an obstacle to cultural penetration.

The most important element of resistance is found in the people, among the poor who have in themselves the greatest potential for change. When the popular sectors achieve levels of organization that permit expression of their own values and self-assertion, they develop an enormous resistive capacity toward external cultural aggression.

In fact, nobody has yet been able to prove that the mass media, with their tremendous technological paraphernalia and persuasive power, can impose values simply by sheer repetition. In most countries, it is not the presidential candidates who spend the most money on publicity campaigns who win elections. In Uruguay in 1980 the full brunt of the communications media was brought to bear on the electorate to vote for the constitutional reform proposed by the incumbent regime. Uruguayans opposed to this choice were not given access to the mass media. However, the Uruguayan people voted massively against the proposal of the dictatorship, and defeated it.

It is clear, and easily demonstrable in the reality of the countries of the Third World, that in spite of the conflict of interests at the economic, social, and political levels, which set the people against the ruling classes (a fact that constitutes in itself a defensive barrier against cultural aggression), there are also deep contradictions within the popular sectors. We find urban and rural workers who, having adopted the values of the consumer society as their own, see their frustration increased by the enormous distance that separates them from the proposed model.

However, other social sectors, especially the middle classes, more openly assimilate these models. This social group and the transnational power that controls the communications media often have similar interests. In Latin America, clothing fashions imposed by big business and keenly followed by the middle classes meet strong resistance from the populous sectors. They tend to keep to their own traditions.

I do not deny the persuasive capacity of the media propaganda put out by the ruling transnational classes. My point is simply that its power is overestimated and should be divested of its mythical irresistibleness that, according to some, would leave an invaded culture practically defenseless.

Similarly, I reject the simplistic notion that one can find in the values of transnational culture all that is bad as opposed to the good of national culture, as if the latter remained unchanged, unmodified throughout time. Some critics support this view in their concern to define the essence of "national culture." But then they often fall back on what is ancestral or folkloric in their attempt to find out who they really are.

Nor is it simply a matter of accepting or rejecting the media. Even if accepting cultural invasion implies acceptance of domination and lack of criticism, total rejection is not possible in the present state of development of the communications media. By the same token, the media condition national culture, which makes it practically impossible for traditional cultures to survive, closed in on themselves. Culture is necessarily dynamic, changing, as are interpersonal relationships generally.

The integration of certain values from transnational culture does not inevitably mean that national culture takes second place. Within certain parameters, the transnational can enhance the indigenous.

Starting with this element of resistance, from dialogue between cultures, and the search for a new identity, interesting perspectives for so-called alternative communication open up, an option that I shall deal with later on.

Communication and Crosscultural Domination

It has been said that "the strategy of transnational domination attempts to impose on our peoples the habits, values, and customs that will neutralize their will for change. Cultural domination is reinforced by the ruling elites as a way of justifying social injustices and the status quo" (Embú, no. 12).

This strategy tries, by means of concerted action in the political, economic, social, and cultural fields, to destroy popular values, the values that a people redeems and revalidates by its deeds, because they are part of the national being and are at the basis of creative abilities that must be reinforced and encouraged in the heart of the people.

There is a confrontation here, within the framework of civil society, in which it is clearly seen that hegemony falls into the hands of transnational ruling power, but from which it is not possible to conclude to either the impotence or the absolute subordination of the people. In this confrontation, communication and information become the decisive fields of struggle.[10]

In the strategy of transnational domination, communication and information are not considered as assets of society in general, but as "the mercantile enterprise of a minority. Their purpose, essentially, is to strengthen established values and neutralize the popular will for change" (Embú, no. 14).

The case of information flow is a convenient example: besides being the most widely studied, it is also the one that most clearly shows the prevailing imbalance in communications. In spite of having been exposed and denounced, the imbalance in information flows and the concentration of information in the hands of a few transnational news production and distribution centers have not changed. This is because global conditions have not improved in favor of greater justice and participation by poorer countries in international affairs and the distribution of wealth, and because of the lack of a clear political will on the part of peripheral countries to defend their own rights. The situation of information imbalance remains as stagnant as when it was denounced at the beginning of the 1970s.

Moreover, the centers of transnational power, not without a measure of cynicism, have come to accept a global diagnosis that demonstrates adverse conditions in the poorer countries. And there is no will for change. On the contrary, developed countries, with the power they command, have chosen to obstruct all the alternatives proposed—albeit without much coherence or conviction—by Third World countries.

Paradoxically, proposals for change have been used as a pretext for introducing new technology in communication—technology that does not contribute to the processes of liberation of the people and constitutes in fact a new instrument of domination. This technological reinforcement, extraneous to national plans for development and ignoring the history of each country, benefits only the transnational corporations. It impedes national economics and cultural indigenous development, and becomes a new means of reinforcing domination.

The introduction of color television in most Latin American countries was not the result of a decision forming part of a general policy of communication attuned to the development needs of the given country. In Argentina, for example, the decision was taken under pressure on the occasion of the world soccer championship of 1978, because Argentina needed color transmission to commercialize the event in cooperation with large international agencies. The country was not in a position, either politically or economically, and did not have the necessary communications infrastructure, to make the change. However, the decision was made. Even six years later, Argentina was still unable to repay the foreign loans obtained in order to buy the equipment needed for the championship coverage.

In other Latin American countries, the decision was precipitated by an offer of equipment made by transnational corporations, accompanied by difficulties in the provision of spare parts and materials for black-and-white systems. Of course, the inability of these nations to develop their own technology also contributed. Once equipment was installed, the limitations of each country in making and selling its own productions, and defending itself from cultural penetration, also became more apparent.

My purpose here is not to initiate an antitechnology movement but to plead for the introduction of new technology in line with the plans for the economic, political, social, and cultural development of each nation, so that each country can be in charge of its own integral development. In other words, it is necessary for each country to be able to regulate the introduction of new technologies as a support for renewed cultural development.

Needless to say, these reflections do not amount to an exhaustive analysis of the problem of social communications at present. They are presented simply as clues to give perspective to and to identify the main features that must be taken into account in any diagnosis.

NWICO: A PROPOSAL FOR CHANGE

The domination endured by the poor of the world as a result of oppression by the powerful is a reality that degrades the whole of humankind as such. Hope for equality and justice is at the root of the struggle of every social group for the well-being of its members.

This was the main motive of the countries of the Third World when they called for a New World Information and Communication Order (NWICO), first within the Movement of Non-Aligned Countries and later at the General Assembly of the United Nations.

Human and democratic restoration of underdeveloped countries coincides with a basic Christian orientation: to work for the dignity of human beings in such a way that we can all see each other as brothers and sisters.

More profound diagnoses of the world situation, as also debates and clarifications on the subject of NWICO, have made it more and more evident that information and communication constitute a field where injustices are flagrant, imperating concrete proposals for change.

At no time was the subject of communication and information seen as a problem isolated from the rest of global problems, but as one aspect of global relations that could be the subject of negotiation within the wider framework of the search for justice and equality at all levels of society.

Imbalances in the processing of world information, dominated by only five large transnational agencies, and the elements inherent in cultural invasion, are certainly not separable from the global problems under discussion. However, the specific treatment given to the problems of information and communication, the debate arising around these particular aspects of the general problem, gave way to a focal point in what was given the title New International Information Order (NIIO).

Three Stages in the NWICO Debate

The initial model of NIIO, which in time evolved into NWICO, generally restores to the poor countries their political and cultural independence. To this end it demands the establishment of a free and balanced flow of information and rejects any attempt at cultural colonialism.

Raquel Salinas Bascur, the Chilean researcher, recognizes three stages in the development of the debate on communication in recent years (see "Nuevo orden").[11]

The first stage, from 1973 to 1976, entailed "politico-ideological confrontation," to stir up ideas, starting from the theoretical work of researchers and with the political support of the poor countries. While that was in progress, the governments in developed countries limited themselves to listening to denunciations, "treating them as mere ideological artifacts" (Salinas Bascur, "Nuevo orden").

The second stage in this process, from 1976 to 1979, consisted in accumulating data, much of it empirical evidence, in order to demonstrate that the political and ideological arguments were based on reality. In other words, it was a matter of presenting data in such a way that cultural and informational domination became evident. This second stage disturbed the developed countries in different ways, and ideologico-political confrontation became deeper, leading to the formulation of the most important ideas in the debate on communication up to that time.

Perhaps one of the most significant points in this stage was that confrontation did not take place solely between developed and underdeveloped countries, but also within those countries where the defenders of NIIO found strong opposition from the establishment, from organizations representing businesses, and from all those at the local level who identified themselves with and defended transnational interests in culture and communication.

The third stage followed the publication of the MacBride Report in 1980. It offered a good resumé of the arguments and the debates mentioned above and relaunched, at the same time, a wave of confrontation on the international scene. The report from the MacBride Commission, the result of efforts by sixteen international experts and their assistants made over a period of three years, gives a very precise view of the problem we face, even taking into account the fact that their work has limitations because of the breadth of the task undertaken, the international character of the analysis demanded, and the political and scientific differences among the experts involved.

You will not find in the report a scientific answer to all the problems of modern communication. The work of the experts gathered by UNESCO is fundamentally an inventory of the problems and a resumé of proposed alternatives. It should be seen as the political expression of the arguments about communication and culture at that particular time. The same applies to NWICO, to such a point that the whole package of documentation has been classified as "minutes of the state of confrontation, and not, in any way, scientific analyses or systematic arguments."[12]

The MacBride Report tells the developed countries and the transnationals involved in communications that there is an imbalance in information and that cultural domination is a reality. Discussion is taking place. It is a question of finding ways out of the situation.

Developed countries and transnational corporations seek, by every possible means, to control the plans intended to change this situation, restricting the provisions of technology, training, and bilateral aid. For Third World countries, this strategy which some have denounced as "a Marshall plan for communications," is nothing but a new and sophisticated way of deepening cultural domination and dependence.

At the international and institutional level, struggle takes place within the limits established by the International Program for the Development of Communications (IPDC). It will be against that background that both sides will try to make their point of view prevail, and to direct the plans that will have to be developed.

Still more important than the international is the national level, where each country will have to fight to establish the essential values of NWICO against internal allies of the transnationals and the interests of the North, and in favor of the democratization of culture and communications.

The development of the debate has brought the central premise of NWICO closer: the democratization of communication. At the same time the certainty of the initial premise has been reaffirmed: there can be no democratic communication without a truly democratic society.

The Most Important Need: Democratization of Communication

The central NWICO proposal is for the democratization of communication. In the words of the MacBride Report:

> Democratization is the process whereby: (a) the individual becomes an active partner and not a mere object of communication; (b) the variety of messages exchanged increases; and (c) the extent and quality of social representation or participation in communication are augmented [p. 166].

In a similar vein, but placing more emphasis on the aspects of social integration, is the statement of the final document of Embú in this respect:

> Democracy is above all a fundamental human attitude, expressed in communication by abolishing authoritarian forms and relying on the conscious, organized, and collective action of the oppressed. Pluralistic participation of social sectors should manifest itself in the different levels of the communication process, particularly in the production, distribution, and consumption of cultural goods [no. 26].

By recognizing the role of protagonist played by the oppressed in the democratization of communication, the Embú document stresses an aspect that can go unnoticed in the definition given in the MacBride Report: the democratization of communication and the democratization of society are variables that depend on each other and cannot, therefore, exist in isolation. To democratize communication it is essential to democratize society, and vice versa.

Precisely because "communication unavoidably reflects the nature of social relationships" (Embú, no. 26), it is not possible to have democratic communication within an authoritarian state.[13] The democratization of communication is a task that democratic sectors, popular movements, must assume in the search for more just social relationships among individuals and nations.

We shall not witness the true democratization of communications if unjust situations prevail that contradict assertions made in international conferences.

The democratization of social relations needs to be done at the national and international levels simultaneously. It is not possible to maintain a more balanced and just information flow at the international level, when at the national level persons are denied access to and participation in communications media and, more importantly, in the formulation of democratic policies of communication.

To expose the dualism of some governments (an attitude that has been used as an argument against NWICO by those who, behind the facade of a liberal ideology, represent the interests of transnational corporations and pose as champions of "freedom of expression") is one of the most important tasks for those who work on behalf of a new order in communication.

At the national level the appeal is for *the democratization of power and economic relations*. In other words, NWICO is based on the premise of building a pluralistic and truly sharing society, where the majority participates in decision-making, formulates and implements national policies at all levels, and actually has control of the government and the state apparatus.

It is also necessary to consider the need for democratization of media ownership. At this level it is important to define the problem, in order to counter the argument repeatedly put forward by detractors of NWICO, of having to choose between private and state ownership. This is a false opposition. In the first place, there is a third alternative, that of social ownership, by means of which, without eliminating the concept of private property, social sectors are given control of communication media through representative organizations. These should, however, be kept under the supervision of the state, provided the state ensures the implementation of national policies of communication agreed upon democratically by the different sectors of society. State and private sectors will also coexist within this new pattern, as long as all media are used harmoniously within a national cultural and communicational policy, and as long as that policy is conceived in a truly democratic way.

An indication of the degree of democratization reached will be the level of access and participation that the poor and marginalized have vis-à-vis the media of communication. For this to take place it will be necessary to ensure that the poor and marginalized receive appropriate education to allow them to use the media. Representative organizations (trade-union, neighborhood, community, educational, political groups, etc.) must be truly representative and have access to the media not just to express the feelings of their members, but to participate actively in the establishment of communication policies, in the control of communications media, and in the production, distribution, and consumption of cultural goods.

In short, it can be said that the democratization of communications implies a fundamental change of perspective. It is not just a matter of making sure that communication reflects the interests and views of all social sectors. It is a matter of creating the conditions so that individuals or nations, especially the poorest, are active participants in the process of communication. Communication should be a democratic exercise that contributes to establishing relationships that dignify the individual.

In the Puebla Final Document, the Latin American bishops demand that "the Church must more and more each day become the voice of the dispossessed, even at the risk entailed" (no. 1094). It would be a step forward, in agreement with the priorities of NWICO and the development of ecclesiastical thought, to ask the church to be "the voice of the dispossessed" and to work to secure the right of all persons, especially the marginalized and dispossessed, to form their own opinions and be able to express them freely.

Development and Communication

Development is a goal common to all nations, whatever degree of progress they may have achieved. However, development is a matter of *urgency* for all poor countries, the majority of which are in the Third World.

At a theoretical level It is generally accepted that development should be "total and integrated"—that is to say, that it should involve all aspects of social life and make it coherent. It is also generally accepted that individuals must be at the center of the process of development that contributes to their enhancement.

Unfortunately, experience shows that the opposite is true. Usually Third World countries lack real development policies, and action at nearly all levels takes place in an unconnected and disorderly fashion.

In poor countries, the situation is made worse by the problem of domination. It is vital that development plans protect autonomy vis-à-vis neocolonial powers and transnational corporations, guaranteeing, at the same time, the possibility of self-reliant development on the basis of the dynamic inherent in the material, scientific, and human resources of even a poor country.

Because it is the person who is at the center of the process of development and the only target of its benefits, all plans and tasks should be drawn up within the democratic perspective outlined in this paper.

Communication does not escape the need for integration and articulation within national policies of development. In other words, communication development must be in direct and harmonious relationship with the overall development of a nation. In this respect the MacBride Report notes:

> Since communication is not an autonomous, separate sector, in this domain perhaps more than in others interdependence makes it essential to develop communication policies which are not limited to information, even less to mass media—they have to take into consideration all ways

and means a society needs and can utilize for its overall development purposes. We must not lose sight of the fact that communication policies go hand in hand with those formulated in other fields—i.e., education, culture, and science—and should be designed to supplement them. Communication should interrelate with these other sectors, so as to promote social, educational, scientific, and other services [p. 204].

The development of communication cannot and should not be left to individual initiatives or commercial interest. The lack of a communications policy that includes its own integration in development plans means the mortgaging of an important part of national sovereignty to the transnational centers of power. In other words, those matters not decided by national political entities will be resolved in the executive offices of the transnational corporations involved in communications. This is a point that must be strongly denounced in the face of the statement that "the best policy in communication is the absence of any policy."

A communication policy entails the development of social communications that support a democratic society as well as the development of technical infrastructures. It must plan how to use existing infrastructures, how to create new ones, and how to assimilate and develop a people's own technology, adapting it to the general objectives of development.

No warning can be too strong with respect to the dangers involved for poor countries in giving in to pressures from transnational enterprises regarding decisions that are not a result of political decisions consistent with development planning. This subject is directly linked to the problem of nearly nonexistent national industries in countries of the Third World. This is because communication as a process is expanding continually and can be held back or advanced by the development of support systems (satellites, broadcasting stations, etc.), and because the production and adaptation of these systems depend directly on the economic and political strategy adopted. As an example, it can be shown that it is far more feasible for a country to close its doors to the import of equipment and programs produced abroad, as a measure of political autonomy and cultural assertion, if it has previously taken the economic and political steps to create favorable conditions for the local production of similar equipment, and to stimulate the creation of programs whose distribution will be guaranteed by the state.

The Embú document points out in the specific case of Latin America:

New technologies in the field of communications are being introduced in the name of modernization and other false interpretations of NWICO. But reality indicates that these resources are not intended to provide better understanding between nations, nor do they meet the priorities and needs of the people. This kind of technological modernization benefits transnational corporations, damages national economies, and attacks political sovereignty [no. 15].

New technologies cannot and should not increase the dependence of poor countries on the transnational corporations that provide the products. On the contrary, nations must set very precise limits to govern the import of these technologies, in such a way that they conform to their own plans of development in communications, seeking ways to participate actively in creating and producing new technologies and, at the very least, in adapting imported technologies to local needs.

Seen in this light, communication becomes a fundamental factor of development, for it tends to facilitate the social relationships that lie at the root of development itself. As the MacBride Report puts it:

> "While it is true that communication by itself cannot bring about development, it is also true that inadequate communication renders development slower and more difficult, as well as impeding popular participation" [p. 206].

Participants in Democratic Communication

The process of democratizing communication demands the interacting presence of different kinds of participants, to ensure plurality of participation by all social sectors:
a) *Institutional:* governments and intergovernmental organizations.
b) *The experts:* specialists and researchers in communications and related disciplines who participate in the debate and struggle for the establishment of the new order.
c) *Grass-roots organizations:* community and popular organizations, women's groups, trade unions, political parties, professional organizations, and the churches.
d) The trade unions and professional organizations relating to workers in the culture industry.

Of these four groups, the first two have actively participated in the process of advancing NWICO aims. However the efforts made by governments and intergovernmental organizations cannot by themselves create the kind of truly democratic communication proposed. Both grass-roots organizations and workers in the culture industry have decisive roles to play in achieving the proposed aims.

The democratization of communication demands, therefore, the twofold effort of using communication as a tool to strengthen these "new participants" as well as the implementation of work to increase the awareness of grass-roots organizations and workers in the communication industry as to the basic principles of NWICO and the need to encourage its implementation. The involvement of popular organizations in the struggle for democratization of communication, on the other hand, relates the process of communication to the political plans of the subordinated classes, the privileged subjects of social change.

For the same reason participation by the popular sectors will tend to guarantee the defense of cultural identity largely the possession of the subordinated classes. This participation will not be the result of gracious concessions by the ruling classes or of a "populist" understanding by others involved in the process. It contains the fundamental key to the success of the democratization process. Therefore, participation by the popular sectors cannot be reduced to marginal aspects, but must be made effective by means of intervention in the production and distribution of communications and in the planning and decision-making process in relation to communication policy.

In this way two of the main objectives of democratization as defined in the Embú document will be achieved:

> That the individual moves from being a mere object of communication to being an active element within it—that is to say, that all members of society, especially the worst-off, have free access to and equal opportunity to use information and communication media. That the degree and quality of social representation and participation, including involvement in the production and distribution of messages and in the decision-making process of communication policy and communication planning increase [no. 29].

Education and Communication

At present the popular sectors fulfill, in most cases, the role of passive recipients of communications broadcast by the media, being the main target of transnational, national, and foreign cultural invasion.

It is not surprising, therefore, that when these popular groups develop and broadcast their own communications, they are full of values foreign to their own culture, and that these experiences repeat a pattern of pseudo communication: vertical manipulative, and identical to the one I have been criticizing.

These popular sectors which are in a position to develop truly creative experiences of communication by transmitting material that is culturally and politically revolutionary, are often trapped in the ideologico-political framework forced on them by vertical communication and, at the same time, lack adequate training to develop their own communication abilities. This is a reality and must be an abiding preoccupation of those who plan communication policy.

Training persons to develop their communication abilities and to communicate in terms of their own interests and values is essential to the process of democratizing communication and should be an integral part of national educational plans. There is sufficient experience to demonstrate that it is not enough for the people to have access to the media if those who use them do not know *how* to use them.

Even more important is the need to encourage a process of self-awareness that will allow criticism of the dominant culture, real identification of potentials and values, and reaffirmation of cultural identity. This is true even though culture changes and is modified, just as social relationships change.

To obstruct this process of popular self-awareness is to limit the scope of education to mere training in the use of the media.

All this demands a pedagogical development that educates the popular sectors by exchanging information on social practices. Concretely, it is important that besides having good technical communications through alternative media (popular newspapers, posters, leaflets, radio programs), the inhabitants of a rural region meet in order to have dialogue and direct exchange of experiences, including experiences of alternative communication. This form of communication is "alternative" because of the participants and the contents of the message, which allow the oppressed to break down the barriers imposed on them by transnational cultural domination, to become conscious of their reality in order to express freely their aspirations for change in a coherent plan of action.

At this level, great responsibility falls on communication researchers and specialists, and on workers in the culture industry. A commitment should be expected of them: that they identify with the people and see the process of change from the point of view of the dominated classes. This will empower them to fulfill a twofold mission. The first is that of becoming the voice of the popular sectors. The second is that they feed the process of self-awareness of the popular sectors, which will enable them to consolidate popular awareness and achieve ideological, political, and cultural identification with the subordinated masses. This process of identification with the popular sectors is an integral part of the task of building a new leadership that will make the democratization of society possible.

It is not enough that researchers, journalists, and those in the culture industry lend themselves to the service of the popular movement. They must work intensively to promote collective consciousness and the ability to communicate. It is not enough to announce through the mass media the restoration of rights. It is necessary to go deeper into the process of becoming conscious of the historical movement toward liberation and the development of communication abilities, so that, aware of the whole process and of the right to communicate, the popular sectors will be able to exercise those rights democratically.

Alternative Communication: An Integral Part of Social Change and Human Development

The NWICO concept gained support mainly through the theoretical work of communication researchers and the political work that gained the backing of poor countries, precisely because they recognized communication as one of the facets of domination.

The debate about NWICO continues at the level of intergovernmental confrontation, and it is difficult to appreciate that popular sectors, grass-roots movements, and political organizations recognize in it their own vindication, a demand that is a part of the struggle for cultural identity and, consequently, for liberation.

Something totally different happened in the case of alternative communication. Long before it had any status in the minds of researchers or politicians, alternative communication was already a part of the experience of the dominated sectors in different parts of the world. These communication experiments are the result of a people's search to find new forms of access to and participation in society. These experiments were not inspired by NIIO or NWICO but, in general terms, they coincide with their fundamental principles.

These new experiments in communication, born within popular movements, trade unions, rural groups, marginal urban dwellers, grass-roots communities and churches, share the characteristic of encouraging nonvertical communication that expresses the feelings and aspirations of the group putting them into practice. They also serve the purpose of communicating between themselves and relating them to other social sectors. These experiments—called group, horizontal, participatory, popular, or grass-roots communication—have now come to be called alternative communication.

Alternative communication has become an instrument favoring political struggle, vindication of rights, and religious concerns. But it has unfortunately retained an almost "underground" character, hardly integrated into the new global perspective of culture and communication. We should analyze it, discover its implications, and evaluate its contribution to the general process of the transformation of society. It is important to do so, and to question some statements that, ignoring this basic datum of grass-roots communication, have reduced the concept to secondary features.

The Latin American political process has linked the concept of alternative communication to the experiences of persons who are searching for new ways to express themselves and for tools they can use in effective political struggle for social change. The pastoral work of the church has had great influence, especially among grass-roots communities, in promoting this new communicative practice.

The genesis of alternative communication in Latin America, the function it has within the political and social process, distinguishes it from what is called alternative communication in developed countries—modes of communication adopted by ghettos or socially marginal groups: minorities in general. Points of contact can be found between both experiences, but they are different because of the different social dynamics in their origins. In Latin America, alternative communication can be appropriately defined only from the point of view of the poor, who make it a tool for human improvement and social change.

For this reason, alternative communication cannot be taken as a "self-defined phenomenon":

It is defined by the political context, and determined by the will for change that seeks to change oppressive structures to create a development model involving solidarity, participation, and democracy in all social sectors.[14]

That is the reason why some authors and the Embú document emphasize the "alternative" aspect (from "alteration," change), which this kind of communication makes evident. It is a response from the people, confronting different forms of oppression and demonstrating the will of the people to do away with domination. This is the fundamental concept of alternative communication which is different from the "other face" of present-day communication, which seems to be implied by the MacBride Report when it recognizes the existence of and refers to alternative communications and counter information.

It must be admitted that the treatment of the MacBride Report on this point is scant inasmuch as it takes this kind of communication to be more of a corrective to deficiencies in present communications than a genuine alternative. It focuses on alternative communications in their "opposition to the influence of predominant information (institutionalized communication used to perpetuate the juridical structure of a society)." It notes that the various forms of alternative communication "oppose the socially, culturally, and politically hegemonic forms of communication."[15]

It is true that alternative communication often appears in this light, because those who control the media refuse to allow access to and participation by the oppressed sectors in institutionalized communication. However, alternative communication is not simply a reaction to lack of access and participation. To think so would be to ignore the fact that those who promote this kind of communication are expressing their will for change, revealing their interests, and establishing a basis on which to construct a democratic, participatory, just, and communal alternative.

The experiences of those who engage in alternative communication differ greatly from one another, and it is therefore impossible to describe them in general terms without losing much of the richness involved in each of them. A much more meticulous investigation of these forms of communication should be made worldwide.

Alternative communication is different because:
  a) The popular sectors, through grass-roots organizations, trade union and professional organizations, political parties and churches, among others, are the subjects of communication.
  b) In many cases, the kind of horizontal communication established becomes two-way, especially as awareness of cultural identity increases.
  c) The content of what it communicates is liberative—an expression of a people living under oppression, actively pursuing change.

The distinctiveness of alternative communication does not depend on the means used: it can be handmade, mechanical, or electronic; it can reach a very small, a medium-range, or a very large audience. The important factor is that it is used by democratic sectors for the purpose of introducing change.

Thus conceived, alternative communication is not merely an instrument to produce social change, but an integral part of the process itself. It reinforces its alternative character the more it strengthens the process of making persons aware of their de facto situation of domination, their potential for producing change, and their cultural identity.

If this does not take place, projects called alternative communication do not deserve the name. They are simply replications of the vertical and manipulating forms of the prevailing modes of communication. However, it is only fair to recognize that this often comes about because of the degree of marginality, if not secrecy, in which these experiments appear and develop, in an environment of repression and political suspicion.

Many so-called alternative communication projects do nothing but reproduce, in a different style, the basic scheme of pseudo communication in which recipients continue to be passive and manipulated. In not just a few cases, experiments in alternative communication reproduce the same forms, language, and vices of the commercial media, precisely because the system of cultural invasion has managed to ingrain them in the popular mind. As the MacBride Report puts it:

> The use value of information spread by alternative networks must be demonstrated, and the mechanisms for users to be transformed into generators of information must be created. Although there are remarkable examples of the creation of alternative networks, these efforst still put excessive emphasis on the production and dissemination of information. The ways for recipients to change into users and producers are not sufficiently clear and without that, it is not possible to talk about either real or alternative communication [p. 297].

Certain experiments in popular participation in mass-media communication are likewise nonalternative, such as have been proposed in schemes typical of the dominant media. To accept that this is a viable possibility would be to set aside the fundamental belief that the problem of domination is at the basis of the contradiction between vertical communication and alternative communication.

Two conditions establish whether a communication experience is really alternative: (1) each of the participants in the process can recognize the message produced as their own; (2) underlying the entire process, the truly democratic principles of equality and participation are respected.

Alternative communication is not restricted to the autonomous environment created by popular movements in their liberation struggles. On the contrary, a coherent approach demands the extension of the alternative experiment to all other levels of the culture industry. This implies developing alternative experiments in fields where popular sectors have to face confrontations with those who hold power, as is the case with new technologies and information science (informatics).[16]

In this respect the final document of the Latin American seminar on communication and pluralism, quoted above, recognizes three aspects of alternative communication:

a) *alternative media*—creation of, and in solidarity with, the popular sectors;
b) *alternative message*, present in alternative media as well as in "breaches" of the prevailing industrial cultural system;
c) *alternative consumption*, or *critical consumption*—collective reflection within grass-roots and popular organizations on the media and their message.[17]

Recognizing the sum of these aspects as the whole phenomenon of alternative communication differentiates it from "marginal communication." The latter term refers to grass-roots, participatory communication that manages to create its own space for communication, reproducing the ideal characteristics of the communication process, but with no chance of making a real impact for social change.

The recognition of different aspects of alternative communication assumes the existence of levels of coordination and articulation, permitting the adoption—within the same global, political, and cultural framework—of small experiments undertaken with simple means by popular sectors, as well as of large-scale projects to create international networks of information with a high level of technological sophistication. In some cases the greater value will be in nearness to the people, direct contact with its most deeply felt aspirations, and greater freedom for creative expression. In others, values should be measured in terms of the wider ambit of influence and animation for taking control of the means of production of the culture industry.

It is a great challenge for Latin America to articulate alternative experiments at the level of large networks, such as those that the agency IPS-Third World develops and encourages, or the one planned in concert with the Latin American Agency for Special Information Services (ALASEI), and others with less influence but deeper popular roots, such as the alternative communication of ecclesial grass-roots communities, popular communication in marginal zones, or the work of circulating information among trade unions, as takes place in some countries.

For the creation and consolidation of such networks of articulation between different experiments, the support of communication professionals in their capacity as intellectuals at the service of the people ("organic intellectuals") is fundamental—not simply as auxiliary technicians but as qualified coparticipants in alternative communication.

As has already been pointed out, many of the experiments called alternative communication do not have all the characteristics given here. There are even fewer alternative networks with the capacity to articulate different kinds of communication, offering the possibility of a communication policy that is both *democratic* and *alternative*. But the steps taken to date make it possible to visualize these new perspectives, and to make sure that alternative communication appears as an interesting possibility within the struggle to place communication at the service of integral human liberation. But this still needs greater theoretical development and political work.

CHURCH AND COMMUNICATION: PASTORAL RESPONSES

Among the outstanding characteristics of Christians in Latin America during the past three decades has been the concern of many to join in the processes of change, through initiatives that come from the people in the continual search for fairer conditions of life, especially for the poorest. This attitude has its counterpart: there are also those who, far from understanding this prophetic perspective, choose to cling to the present situation because it brings certain benefits to them. But, as the Latin American bishops agreed at Puebla:

> The Church has been acquiring an increasingly clear and deep realization that evangelization is its fundamental mission; and that it cannot possibly carry out this mission without an ongoing effort to know the real situation and to adapt the gospel message to today's human beings in a dynamic, attractive, and convincing way [no. 85].

The experiences of Christians in the field of communications sprang from this pastoral attitude, marked by the same prophetic symbols and contradictions that permeate the whole church. As a result, in communication matters and as a logical demand of its mission—evangelization—the church is faced with a twofold challenge: reality that demands prophetic pronouncements, and NWICO as a possibility for change and as an alternative to the present situation.

The response to both challenges should agree with the option taken by the Latin American church, and repeatedly ratified by its bishops, in favor of the poor. To agree with this option means taking the perspective of, considering history from the point of view of, and starting from the needs of the poor, as well as a basic commitment to the task of liberation.

In fulfilling its mission of evangelization, the church adopts different pastoral responses with respect to communication, its problems and perspectives, according to different circumstances and the basic attitude assumed by Christian communities and by pastoral ministers. Different responses coexist in the Latin American church, within each national church, and even within a given local community. That is the logical result of different developments of awareness in the face of historical reality and of training in communications on the part of Christians.

It seems useful to review certain pastoral responses to communication, past and present, given by the Latin American church. What follows is a (perhaps as such oversimplified) listing of characteristics, certainly not a definitive typology.

Self-Defense

Rather than a pastoral response, this is a self-protective attitude vis-à-vis the communication media and their message. Communication is reduced to the instrumental level, without even understanding its language.

This position can still be found among those Christians who maintain the apologetic attitude that the church is the sole possessor of truth, which it should spread. From the viewpoint of this starting point, it is easy to understand the need felt to counteract mistakes made by the media and, as far as possible to prevent such mistakes. In fact, those who support this position advocate censorship or even intervention on the part of the state, and demonstrate total contempt for the communication media as a vehicle for evangelization.

This attitude corresponds to, and confirms, the vertical understanding of intrachurch communication.

Apostolic Conquest

This attitude is based on essentially the same ecclesiatical certitude as the preceding: the church is the only possessor of truth. However, the pastoral response is different: Christians demand an opportunity to spread the truth they possess. Communication as such is still limited to its instrument level, but those who adopt this position take care to learn the techniques and language of the media.

As a pastoral response, the principle at work here is: to oppose good media to bad media, good message to bad message. Those who maintain this position concentrate most of their pastoral efforts in the field of communication on encouraging the appearance of specifically Catholic media, dependent either on the hierarchy or at least on Catholic management. Simultaneously they seek to unite Catholics employed in the mass media in order to work out "good themes" with them and contribute to public opinion favorable to the church and its apostolic mission.

There is no major preoccupation with communication within the church. This favors continuation of the vertical, undirectional sytle, which, in essence, negates communication.

Critical Training

The starting point here is a basic attitude substantially different from the previous one, inasmuch as the usefulness of the communication media and the contribution they can make to a society as a whole are explicitly recognized coupled with a critical attitude vis-à-vis the disruptive influence they can have.

One of the fundamental insights here is that to forbid error does not necessarily prevent it. But it is also understood that the communication media can play an important role in human development.

In this pastoral perspective there are two versions of the concept of evangelization: (1) human development and evangelization are two separate tasks, (2) social work is an integral part of evangelization. The communication work of those who maintain the latter version is characterized by great efforts in the training of recipients, those to whom communications are directed.[18] What is wanted is active criticism, for which recipients must be trained. Great emphasis is put on critical training, even if it reaches Catholic communication professionals more than the general public or pastoral ministers who work in fields other than communication.

In Latin America the moment of greatest success of this pastoral position came with the appearance of several Catholic radio stations conceived as radio schools and directly linked to literacy and development work in poverty-stricken rural areas.

This pastoral radio presence, besides making a decisive contribution toward human development, constituted the most serious commitment of the church in the area of communication and served as a platform for committed and creative action in this field.

Group Communication

Technological advances and a lowering of the cost of small equipment made available to those engaged in pastoral ministry a whole range of communication resources—cassettes, audiovisual aids, videotapes, and so forth. A whole new field opened up for these media, which are economical and easy to use. And their use led to the discovery of a methodology of group work, called "group communication," which meant other media and resources of communication could also be used—theater, leaflets, and even the mass media. The church found in these "mini media" or "poverty media," as they were called at one time, an important pastoral alternative for its work in communication. Latin America became a pioneer in group communication. Catechists and educators led the way, many of them working among the poor.

Group media have been defined as "resources or instruments that, because of their nature and mode of use, open the way to communication and creativity in group form."[19] Those who commit themselves to communication tasks from this perspective develop group techniques and methodologies to a high degree. In general terms, pastoral workers want to encourage the masses to look at reality critically and join in the work of liberation. For this reason, group communication is widely used in pastoral work, where step by step it evolves toward popular communication—that is, toward the need for the popular sectors to use these elementary media to express themselves.

The proposal to use mini media is made on the basis that they lend themselves to evangelization because they "foster education in depth and, in that sense, have an irreplaceable function," and they are preferable to the mass media, which "seem less suitable for conveying Christian doctrine in its entirety and for eliciting conscious, free, and personal choice."[20]

Those who turn to the possibilities offered by the mini media show in some way their dissatisfaction with the global reality of communication as a social fact, channeling into their own work their frustration over the position of the church on the sidelines in the mass media world. This attitude evolves slowly toward favoring group communication. They place little emphasis on its technical aspects, and pursue a broader goal—that of methodologically moving toward the broader achievement of authentic communication by the individual and the group.

Group communication, making use of "poverty media," is based on theological and pastoral reflection characterized by a commitment to the poor. It opens the door to a broader concept of the socio-cultural world. Group communication creates conditions for a better and deeper understanding of the subject of communication and opens up possibilities for more active participation by Christians in the search for solutions at the global level.

Communication for Liberation

As they deepen their commitment to the people, Latin American Christians also advance in their understanding of the historical process and of the role the poor play in that process, not as individual subjects but as a social category mandated to be a fundamental part of the transforming dynamism of society. This promotes greater involvement of Christians in popular struggles. In some instances—in Brazil and Central America, for example—new organizations at the service of popular interests have emerged from the church.

There is an explicit recognition that the social task is an integral part of the following of Christ, and that, therefore, commitment to women is inseparable from evangelization. In this context, communication is rediscovered as a social relationship, forming an integral part of the historical process, which is the very basis of culture and constitutes a fundamental part of the struggle for liberation.

Experiences emerge from the pastoral practice of the church—such as those of grass-roots ecclesial communitites—that are very important from the point of view of communication because they offer possibilities for communication by the people, they are sources of creativity and new forms of communication expressive of Christian liberation, and, as part of the social process, grass-roots ecclesial communities generate alternative communication. This new perspective replaces the instrumentalist view of communication.

This development creates favorable conditions for two lines of work, until now separate, to meet: that of professionals who work at the level of the mass media, and that of pastoral workers involved in group or popular communication. Convergence takes place mainly at the theoretical level: a disposition to accept NWICO as the main point of conceptual reference, and emphasis on Christian commitment that takes the side of the poor and is orientated toward Christian liberation.

However, this theoretical convergence is not verified in practice. The points of agreement within a global pastoral strategy in the field of communication are not very clear. It must be said, though, that the problem is basically the same that arises when the attempt is made to integrate alternative communication into a policy of communication at the national or regional level.

It may be worth pointing out that work in the mass media constitutes a profession, whereas those who work in group communications are professionals in other disciplines (educators, politicians, etc.), who resort to the media in the search for greater effectiveness in their specific tasks.

Church-affiliated radio stations and some print media seem, to date, the most fertile ground for this new pastoral synthesis. This kind of communication, especially that linked to grass-roots church communities, starts to generate new lines of communication within the church. The vertical, unidirectional bearing of church communications is questioned. Unfortunately, at the hierarchical level understanding of the problems of communication and of the new challenges presented to the church, even with respect to its own internal communication, is lacking. There is the danger of impending crisis due to this lack of understanding of the attitudes that pastoral workers might adopt.

PROPOSALS FOR ACTION

Everything that has been stated so far constitutes a challenge to the church:

Our faith prompts us to discern the summonses of God in the signs of the time; to bear witness to, announce, and promote the evangelical values of communion and participation; and to denounce everything in our society that runs counter to the filiation originating in God the Father and the brotherhood rooted in Jesus Christ [Puebla, no. 15]

The church, affected by this reality of communication, must look for answers pertinent to the present time.

Understanding Communication as an Inseparable Part of the Social Process

For many Christians this is a new dimension of communication, going far beyond the instrumentalist approach used for so long.

In view of the evangelical option for the poor, and what this demands in terms of commitment to justice and fellowship to make communion and participation in a democratic and pluralist atmosphere possible, the church faces a twofold prophetic challenge. All its means and resources, backed by the moral weight of the ecclesiastical institutions, must be used, "regardless of the risk incurred" (cf. Puebla, no. 1094), to denounce the domination to which human beings are subjected, including that of communication systems. Simultaneously, the work of announcing the kingdom of God must be undertaken, placing the resources of the church at the service of human development and liberation.

For this undertaking to be genuine, it is necessdary to ensure that participation by different social sectors in the production, distribution, and consumption of cultural goods be deomcratic and pluralist, according to principles of communion and participation, especially guaranteeing the poor and marginalized their right to communication.

Working for Cultural Creativity

To the extent that the challenge sketched just above has become an attitude toward life among Latin American Christians working in communication, they have understood the need to participate actively in the task of cultural creativity and the production of media material. However, this task is still a great challenge for the majority of church personnel working in the field of communication. Such a presence in cultural productivity seeks to evangelize human cultures "not in a purely decorative way as it were by applying a thin veneer, but in a vital way, in depth and right to their very roots" (*Evangelii Nuntiandi*, no. 20).

Consequently we must recognize that the values and cultural norms of most popular sectors are those that give origin to the cultural context and are the basis of collective awareness.

In its task of evangelization, the church must assist the popular sectors in the production and distribution of themes. These new themes must create not only content but also form, adapting both to the objectives sought. Particularly in countries in Latin America and others in the Third World where there are high levels of repression and censorship that impede the production and distribution of such communications, the church must contribute, lending its own structures to create opportunities for freedom and sharing so that such communication can be produced, distributed, and used. In this work the church should not overlook any means at its disposal. The church should also encourage Christian communication professionals to identify themselves more and more with the values inherent in popular culture, putting its technical capacities into the promotion of themes originating from within populous sectors, helping them to have greater impact on the whole of the society.

Promoting Networks of Alternative Communication

Alternative communication networks, understood as the sum of alternative media, themes, and products, constitute a sign of hope in the search for fairer and better conditions for human life.

The Latin American church has developed important alternative communication networks, especially through processes of communication worked out by grass-roots communities. It is a challenge for the church to encourage such experiences of alternative communication and the networks that link them, and especially to enhance articulation of group communication, popular communication, and certain work being done in the mass media.

It is important that the Latin American church systematize these experiences in order to share them with other churches, and with popular organizations, unions, and political parties, so as to help strengthen organizations that represent the people and that contribute to the struggle for a new society. It should share these experiences with government officials responsible for elaborating communication policies in each country. Here the church should take more interest—influencing, encouraging, analyzing, and acting—so that the communication policy of each country really meets the needs and aspirations of the population.

Educating for Communication

Education and training are still high-priority tasks in the pastoral work of the church in communication.

In need of such training are, in the first place, the great majority of pastoral workers who are not specialists in communication and who are far from understanding the complex problems of modern communication as a sociocultural, technological, and pastoral phenomenon. This includes all those who devote themselves to the task of evangelization and have responsibilities, hierarchical or other, within the church.

Such training must try to facilitate understanding communication as an inseparable art of socio-historical reality, and evangelization as an authentic process of communication. It should also publicize development of new experiences along the general lines of NWICO.

The task of education includes working with the popular sectors in strengthening their self-awareness, awakening their communicative potential, and providing adequate technical instrumentation so that they can communicate in an authentic, efficient, and unhampered way. It also implies discerning the authentic values of the people to encourage a shared process of creation of new languages, themes, and contents, suited to proposed objectives.

Christian communication professionals must take part in this activity. As a result of their work for the popular sectors they will be better able to identify, understand, and assess the values of the people—values that will be reviewed from the point of view of new objectives reformulated in group practive. This duty of Christian professionals involves pastoral commitment and human and spiritual rapprochement toward those Christians who feel left out by the church.

Finally, the task of educating imposes parallel research that will diagnose problems and propose alternatives for overcoming them—alternatives that will emerge from social practice. In order to fulfill this task, the church must work closely with those professional nondenominational organizations that specialize in communication research, in order to undertake joint activities that will be mutually beneficial.

Reviewing Communication by and in the Church

The good news must be proclaimed in the first place by witness—"witness which involves presence, sharing, solidarity, and which is an essential element, and generally the first one, in evangelization" (*Evangelii Nuntiandi,* no. 21). The challenge of solidarity—evangelization by witness—is one of the greatest.

The church, which announces the gospel and finds in the ideas of NWICO a number of elements capable of helping its members grow in justice and fellowship, must show in its own institutional structure that it is capable of putting these ideas into practice. The first challenge of democratization, participation, and dialogue comes from within the church itself. There is a long way to go in this respect, especially in the understanding of authority as service, of more active participation by the whole people of God in the decision-making process, and in the shared exercise of authority.

Some steps have already been taken in this direction. One example is that of Catholic organizations working in communication, such as OCIC and UNDA. They oblige us to strengthen, institutionally, our commitment to dialogue, democratic participation, and freedom of expression within the church. New forms of communion and sharing within the church can be found in grass-roots ecclesial communitites. These communities offer the church new models of communication that should be taken into account when assessing the advance of the people of God and its institutional life.

Church communication should not exhaust itself within its own confines. It should extend to ecumenical dialogue with other Christian churches, sharing with them common tasks in the quest for liberative communication, as an expression of fidelity to Jesus Christ, who desires unity among those who believe in him.

The criteria for dialogue and participation should also be taken into account in the liturgy, "privileged moment of communion and participation for evangelization that leads to authentic integral liberation" (Embú, no. 38), in such a way that the lowly can authentically express their feelings in praise and adoration, and celebrate the gift of life.

Probably the greatest challenge faced by the church, as a challenge to its solidarity and as proof of its commitment to the aims of NWICO, would be the establishment of its own communications network. This would help local churches to put into practice their own plans for pastoral care. Communication media could give effective support to a two-way, balanced flow of information that would allow greater participation by everyone in the formulation of pastoral plans, which are at the same time effective as a means of evangelization.

NOTES

1. DECOS-CELAM, *Evangelización y comunicacíon social en America Latina*, Bogotá, Paulinas, 1979.

2. Ibid., p. 49.
3. Ibid., p. 48.
4. Final Document of the Third General Conference of the Latin American Episcopate; English translation in *Puebla and Beyond,* John Eagleson and Philip Scharper, eds., Maryknoll, N.Y., Orbis, 1979, pp. 123-285.
5. See the apostolic exhortation *Evangelii Nuntiandi,* Dec. 8, 1975; English translation, *On Evangelization in the Modern World,* Washington, D.C., U.S. Catholic Conference, 1976.
6. The final report takes its name from the chairman of the commission, Séan MacBride; published by UNESCO, 1980.
7. See *Cultura, evangelización y vida religiosa,* Bogotá, CLAR, 1981, pp. 16-19.
8. Meeting organized by UNDA-LA, SAL-OCIC, UCLAP, and UCBC, Oct. 8-12, 1982 for social scientists, communication professionals, and pastoral workers, with the object of making a global study of the church and NWICO.
9. Heriberto Muraro, *La invasión cultural en América Latina,* Buenos Aires, July 1982.
10. "If hegemony means the maintenance of the cohesion and directioning of society by means of ideologico-cultural action, it is evident that no combination of social forces in contemporary society will ever achieve it except with the help of the most efficacious kind of ideologico-cultural diffusion" (Carlos Eduardo Lins da Silva, *Comunicação, hegemonia e contra-informação,* São Paulo, Cortez, 1982, p. 18).
11. Raquel Salinas Bascur, "Nuevo orden informativo: balance y perspectiva," *UNDA-AL Comunicación,* no. 7, Bogotá, Nov. 1982, pp. 28-37.
12. Rafael Roncagliolo, "EL NOMIC: comunicación y poder internacional," Lima, June 1982.
13. "Inequalities in wealth distribution inevitably create disparities between those who are well-served and those who are deprived in communication: a gap between a cultural elite and illiterate or semi-literate masses is a gap between the information-rich and the information-poor; and an undemocratic political system cannot fail to have adverse effects on communication" (MacBride Report, p. 166).
14. Gilberto Gimeniz, "Notas para una teoria de la comunicación popular," *Christus,* 517 (Mexico City, Nov. 1978): 30.
15. Seminario Latinoamericano, "Comunicación y pluralismo: Alternativas para la década," Final Document, Mexico City, Nov. 1978, no. 2.
16. "A dualist vision of power and domination often impedes the setting up of 'alternatives' in the socio-political 'spaces' in dispute, and not only in the 'autonomous' spaces created and controlled by subordinated classes. New technologies, informatics, and national and international networks of communication often appear as forbidden spaces in alternative discourse. The same discourse glorifies small media and local and isolated experiments, without even querying the way those media and experiments can be and are conditioned by global developments in communications" (Alfredo Paiva, *Por una información libre y liberadora,* Lima, CELADEC, 1982, p. 10).
17. "Comunicación y pluralismo," no. 8.
18. Pope Paul VI, in the pastoral instruction *Communio et Progressio,* touches on this pastoral attitude when he points out that "recipients will generally play an active part if they correctly interpret communications, judging and evaluating them according to their source and context, if they are gathered with care and a critical spirit, if—when necessary—they complement information received with information obtained from

other sources, and if they do not hesitate to show openly their acceptance, reservations, or disapproval" (no. 82).

19. Jacques Cosineau, ed., *Audiovisuales y evangelización,* Lima, El comité organizador, 1978, p. 45.

20. Seminario de Responsables Continentales de Comunicación, final document (Santa Ines, Oct. 1966), in Benito Spoletini, *Comunicación social e Iglesia,* (Bogotá, Paulinas, 1977, p. 41.)

CHAPTER SIX

Christians Building a New Order of Communication

Robert A. White

We are living today in the midst of a historic, worldwide change in the perception of how human communication should be structured. It can best be described as a shift from a more vertical, authoritarian, didactic form to a more participatory, dialogical, horizontal pattern. This shift is observable in Third World nations and in developed industrial countries. It is being discussed by international and national bodies, in local communities, and in families or groups of friends. The movement toward a New World Information and Communication Order (NWICO) is but one aspect of this long-term shift.

Many Christians see in this the realization of their own gospel values, but they ask, "What can I do about it?" Those of us who are communication professionals agree that Third World countries should have more news about their own countries and that they should be making their radio and television programs in their own countries. We agree that the poor and minorities in all countries should have more access to the media and should participate in the making of media policies. We question the control of our communications by large transnational corporations. As Christians we support communication that respects the dignity, creativity, and freedom of every person. But all of this seems so distant from our own concerns as ecclesiastical directors of communication, directors of centers producing audiovisual aids, or directors of pastoral communication training centers. We feel that we can have no influence on national communication policies and even less influence on far-off UNESCO meetings.

Since the 1960s most churches have set in motion a process that has implications not just for the content of communications but also for the participatory structure of communication. There is a greater voice for the local church and small Christian communities are encouraged. Lay persons have a more important role, and there is an increasing variety of ministries. There is a much broader base for collegial decision-making that involves all sectors of the church. A respect for local cultures and the inculturation of the church is growing. There is deep questioning of the triumphalist trappings of feudal power and a clear option for a church "poor with the poor." But as persons responsible in some way for how the church uses the media or how dioceses and parishes communicate, we are often not too sure how these changes should translate into actual communication practices. It is easy to fall back on models offered by the secular society around us or to continue using the tried-and-true-models of an earlier church period.

Christians are much better at giving living witness to the gospel than at thinking up new theories or policies. In our hearts we are convinced that a new communication order is not going to come about simply by the decisions of ministers of state or by discussions of UNESCO experts, as important as these may be. Rather, a new order will be the fruit of hundreds of ordinary decisions of persons with ordinary responsibilities for the way we communicate. In all our ordinary decisions we are faced with options that may have significant implications for new patterns of communication.

QUESTIONS, OPTIONS, DECISIONS

Suppose you are the director of a Christian communication center and you want to provide audiovisual materials for group communications. You wonder whether it would be better to import some excellent slide-cassette sets better than you could ever produce locally or whether to encourage local groups to produce their own material that would capture local images and symbols much better but would be technically less impressive.

The local broadcast station has offered you the opportunity to present a Christmas program, but has made it clear that the program should not stress too much the connection between the plight of the poor in your city and the birth of Jesus in poverty. Should you accept the opportunity to give a bland, nostalgic program?

An innovative new community radio station stressing local culture and community participation invites your church to participate. Should you support this futuristic effort or should you play it safe with the established media, although you know that they do not always represent the interests of the poor and minorities?

Your bishop asks you to help set up a diocesan newspaper. What model of a communicating church should it reflect? Should you opt for a newspaper that raises current issues, linking faith with life, and that appeals to persons marginal to the life of the church? Would a newspaper appealing to traditional pieties of loyal Christians and reflecting a more clerical image be less risky?

With your limited time and resources you wonder whether you should emphasize a strategy of small-group communication that would lead to a grass-roots community structure and a deeper questioning of a consumer society—or would it be better to emphasize a mass communication approach appealing to a large number with inspirational programs and general information about the church?

Or suppose you are asked by your bishop to develop radio programming, or perhaps start up a church-related radio station. If it is decided that a radio station be inaugurated, should its administrative structure be controlled by church persons or should you invite wider participation from the community?

You find that most pastors prefer programming that appeals to their middle-class church members. Should the emphasis be on programming for the poor, for minorities, and other groups that almost never have a voice in the media—or any place else?

A good part of your programming will be music. It is much more economical to play the pop records provided by big transnational record companies. The kids want to hear these "hit tunes." They also bring in more advertising revenue to support religious programming. You wonder whether you should risk efforts to develop a public taste for local artists and music that might stimulate deeper questioning.

You want to provide better in-depth news. Should you take a good balance from the international wire services and the national press office, or should you try to get news from alternative news agencies? Should one emphasize that ordinary persons, the poor, make news as well as do powerful regional and national figures?

Or suppose you are the director of a pastoral communication training center. Should you emphasize a high degree of expertise, with the latest media equipment and training by experts who do really professional work in the media? Or would it be better to stress the ability to analyze the culture, language, and symbols of potential audiences in order to focus on them and express them in the most appropriate media?

What model of church and what pattern of communicating in the church will be incorporated in the training? Should training link communication education with issues of faith and justice in any way?

If your training program is in a developed country, should you try to fill up empty places by bringing in persons from the Third World? Or would it be better to fill them with persons from neglected minorities in your own country?

Certainly these are only a sampling of "typical difficult options" one might encounter, and even these present themselves in immensely varied ways in different countries and at different times. There probably are no "right" answers to any of these questions. But it is obvious that different options imply different orders of communication—and different ways of witnessing to the gospel.

Rarely do Christian communicators choose their options for a plan of communication simply on the basis of their idealism. They look around at available models—in the church and in secular society—and they examine the technical and financial possibilities open to them. It is not surprising that often the imagination of Christian communicators is strongly influenced by the structure of secular media. As a result, the content is Christian, but the pattern of communication reflects the values of a commercial, technical society. In the end the message of the institutional organization of church media may speak more loudly than the content.

The very questionable approaches of fundamentalist prime-time preachers, with their computerized letters to the sick and lonely, and their use of image advertising to "sell Christ," are only some of the most notable examples of this. It is difficult for Christian communicators to rise above the cultural complexities in which they live in order to get a broader and more critical perspective of their work. We may look back on the Inquisition with shame, but to those in that cultural world it all seemed reasonable and justified.

Often we find ourselves using a particular model of communication simply because it is what others are doing. One of the beneficial aspects of the NWICO debate is that it makes us probe the historical context in which we live. Historical analysis helps us to rise above the status quo of the present moment and choose our options with a greater consciousness of what is influencing us and how we are influencing persons and events around us. Why are some professionals questioning the present order? Where did these questions originate? What is the movement toward a new order trying to accomplish?

The discussions surrounding the New World Information and Communication Order (NWICO) can be summarized in many ways, but six issues seem to be central:

1) The communications media should serve the interests of all the public, not just the interests of the economically and politically powerful, whether the powerful be individuals, corporations, or countries.

2) Communication is not a process of handing down in didactic fashion the knowledge of an elite, but rather a fostering of horizontal interchange and a mutual fashioning of culture among equals.

3) More decentralized communication systems are needed, allowing broader access to, participation in, and use of these systems.

4) Communication is a human right and communication systems should allow for greater participation in their creation and administration.

5) If the right to communicate is basic, then education to use this right should be an integral part of all education.

6) The authoritarian models of communication implicit in the traditional concept of the science of communication and in public philosophies of communication need to be questioned and radically reformulated.

Many of these issues have a long history in both new and old nations. All of them involve in some way the models of communication that the church uses.

Historical Trend Toward Public Responsibility for the Media

The centuries-long struggle for freedom of the press against various forms of political censorship by autocratic and aristocratic central governments is a well-known fact. Only in the mid-nineteenth century was the libertarian moral principle enshrined in Western liberal democracies, ensuring freedom of expression to anyone who owned a press. The press defined itself as the "Fourth Estate," ready to bring political decisions into the forum of public debate and striving to present a variety of points of view. By the mid-nineteenth century newspapers fronting for political parties gradually gave way to the popular "penny newspaper," which asserted the principle of objective news reporting and representation of the interests of the general public. What was not always stressed, however, in this heyday of laissez-faire economics, was that freedom of expression meant freedom for the owners of the press, not necessarily freedom of the ordinary citizen.

Throughout the nineteenth century there was a steady trend toward the concentration of ownership of the press in the hands of a few great "press barons"—a Hearst in America or the Lords Rothermere and Beaverbrook in Britain. This eventually provoked public reaction.

Through the first half of the twentieth century a new "social responsibility" theory of the media developed: the libertarian principle, linking freedom of expression with ownership, should be counterweighted by public responsibility and some public control. Many countries introduced legal controls or other measures against concentration of ownership. There was better training of newspaper staffs, and self-regulating professional codes to ensure better service to the public. In some countries watchdog press councils with some citizen representation were established. In Europe the new broadcasting media were organized in terms of public corporations or government-related bodies. However, the media generally remained the preserve of a financial or professional elite.

Origin of the NWICO Debate

In the post-World War II period the new nations emerging from former colonial dependencies brought the debate on concentration of media power to the international level. The initial focus was on the international news agencies. Over a period of one hundred years, 1850 to 1950, five international wire services developed within the political spheres of the great imperial nations. British-based Reuters reported news in the British empire. Havas in France covered the nineteenth-century French colonial dependencies. Wolf in Germany (until World War I) covered Eastern Europe. The (American) Associated Press, and later the United Press, gradually extended control over the U.S. sphere of influence in Latin America and then the rest of the world.

These agencies generally reported news primarily of interest to their constituent newspapers in Britain or America. In times of war or political crisis, these news agencies reflected the political interests of their home country. Subscribers to the news services in poorer countries found that all their news was filtered through the perspective of the powerful nations. Often their stage of national development required a quite different approach to news and information. Moreover, the newspaper formats and styles of reporting imitated those of the North Atlantic nations.

With the development of radio, cinema, records, and television, companies in the U.S.A. and a few other countries dominated international cultural marketing. The expansion of the transnational corporations in the 1950s and 1960s introduced the practice of uniform international advertising campaigns to synchronize consumer tastes on a global basis.

The new nations in Asia and Africa, and a Latin America with a new sense of independence, found that their political and economic independence meant little as long as their cultural development was so heavily dominated by North Atlantic nations. Persons living in non-Western cultures, developed over thousands of years, sensed that their traditions were threatened by the cheap, materialistic "throw away" pop culture of the U.S.A. It is important to note that not only Third World countries but nations such as Canada and Australia have also become deeply concerned about this cultural invasion. Cultural extinction was seen as tantamount to the physical death of a people.

Because individual Third World countries were helpless before the power of great industrial nations of the North, they began to seek a united voice in fora such as the nonaligned nations movement, in the United Nations, and in UNESCO. The formation of alternative international news services was an early development. Countries in the nonaligned movement formed a news union based on the structure of Tanjug of Yugoslavia. Interpress Service, based in Rome, has become the largest of the independent alternative international agencies representing Third World interests. Many nations with a stronger sense of national self-determination have enacted laws controlling the imports of television programming and films, and have encouraged their own local production.

In the early stages of the debate in UNESCO, the U.S.S.R. championed the cause of Third World nations under the banner of "national sovereignty." The U.S. control of satellite technology and easy transborder data flow were special concerns. Unfortunately, this confused the NWICO movement with the cold-war conflict and obscured many central issues such as cultural autonomy and more participatory structures.

The confrontation between the U.S.A. and the U.S.S.R. boiled up in the 1976 UNESCO biennial general assembly in Nairobi. As a form of compromise, UNESCO established an international commission headed by Séan MacBride to make a thorough study of the problem and present a report. UNESCO also sponsored a series of regional intergovernmental meetings to develop new guidelines for national communication policies—in San José, Costa Rica (1976), for Latin America; Kuala Lumpur, Malaysia (1979) for Asia; and Yaoundé, Cameroon (1981), for Africa. Out of these meetings came a series of proposals for national self-determination in communication and for protecting cultural autonomy.

However, in the sessions of the MacBride Commission and in other intergovernmental meetings it became increasingly apparent that the solution was not just greater control over cultural imports but the transformation of the models of concentrated media control introduced from North Atlantic countries during previous colonial periods. Latin America had taken over the U.S. model of private ownership of media and often all the major media of a country—press, radio, and television—were dominated by a few powerful families. In Africa and Asia the model was the highly centralized BBC and French broadcasting systems of the 1930s and 1940s.

It was disturbing that in the early periods of the NWICO discussion some right-wing repressive governments gladly supported the principle of "national sovereignty." Greater national self-determination had to be complemented with profound structural changes within countries.

Out of these discussions have come proposals for much more responsibility to the public and much more participatory systems. The media must be open to the voice of popular movements among the poor and marginal populations. Clearly, the central NWICO theme is now participatory, democratic communication systems.

This move toward more participatory communications in the Third World has been joined by similar demands of minority groups in the developed nations. There is now a general feeling that the old libertarian and even the social responsibility models are inadequate. What is needed is a new model of participatory public communication that guarantees more fully the personal right to communicate.

Development of the Principle of the Right to Communicate

There is a long-standing tradition in Western cultures that public communication consists of an enlightened elite instructing the uncultured and the ignorant. It builds on the strong persuasion model of classical oratory and believes it has a responsibility to transmit its own understanding of culture. It is akin to what Paulo Freire has termed the "banking" concept of education in which the ideology of elites becomes the general norm for the rest of the nation. The didactic concept of public communication underlies the policy of some centralized state-related broadcasting systems. In part the extension education programs in rural areas of the United States are based on this concept.

The classic model of mass communication—source→channel→receiver→effects—emphasizes that the process of communication begins with the source and that the information of the source is normative. The purpose of communication is to realize some proposed effect in the relatively passive receiver.

In the post-World War II period, when the great move toward international aid and intensive national development planning in the Third World began to take shape, the model used was the diffusion of modernization from developed to less-developed nations. Not only the technology but also the culture and social organization of North Atlantic nations were to be introduced into developing countries. The process would begin by modernizing the traditional elites in the urban centers of the new nations, forming great centralized development bureaucracies in education, health, agriculture, and so forth.

What was not fully realized was that many of the developing nations had a traditional hierarchical elite→peasantry communication structure. The modernization of the elites transformed the paternalistic relationship of urban and rural elites into an exploitive and economic relationship. Mass communication—in the hands of the elites—was proposed as the best way to rapidly penetrate the villages—and minds—of the rural majority. Basic structural changes such as land reform were ignored because it was thought that information in itself was the solution.

Some of the massive development communication efforts carried provisions for elaborate research to determine if the desired "effect" of making peasants in India or Peru carbon copies of the American middle class was being realized. Research discovered the "information gap"—namely, that better educated, more affluent persons used the information better and that more information without structural change only increased the gap between the information-rich and the information-poor. Often researchers were hesitant to think that information might be irrelevant to the poor. Rather, they blamed the resistance, fatalism, religious traditionalism, or some other psychological problem in the poor and decided that the solution was more ingenious persuasion to break down resistance.

Criticism of the modernization-diffusion model brought forward new perspectives on communication and development:

a) Without structural changes, much of the information beamed at the poor is not only irrelevant but often is aimed at inculcating a dependency on more favored classes and the acceptance of a dominative ideology.

b) The most appropriate pattern of communication does not come from above but arises within popular movements with the language and symbols that the poor themselves create. The pattern of communication in popular movements is much more horizontal and participatory. The most appropriate form of media, often simpler and controlled by the poor, also comes from the grass roots. The pattern of communication at the grass roots is also much more likely to incorporate elements of indigenous cultures. Westernized urban elites, called upon to produce the programs of the mass media, have not infrequently lost contact with the stream of cultural history in their own countries.

Many now think that NWICO is more likely to grow out of the alternative communication of the poorer and marginal groups than from the top-to-bottom national communication planning by experts. The sources of new patterns of communication are to be found in the popular radio stations that are the voice of the voiceless, in small group communication, in popular theater, or in independent documentation centers.

It is significant that many of these alternative communication experiences originated in projects undertaken by Christians in alliance with movements among marginal groups and the poor.

Media Decentralization and Control

Wherever media ownership has been organized in terms of private enterprise, there has been a tendency for a progressive concentration of ownership, unless clear and effective legal controls have prevented it. In the U.S.A., the norm for broadcast licensing initially sanctioned the principle of localism, but local stations found it more profitable to affiliate with national networks for most of their programming. In Europe, for technical, political, and cultural reasons, broadcasting was originally organized in independent national corporations or as a department of the government. In former British and French areas of colonial influence in Africa and Asia, where the model of a national broadcasting system has been introduced along British or French lines, administration is located within a branch of government.

Some nations have favored centralization of public media in order to foster national integration and to reduce costs. Conditions vary, but generally these forms of concentration of control have tended to reduce diversity in content, open up the possibility of political influence, and lessen the opportunity for public access and participation.

Since the mid-1960s, there has been a broad movement toward more decentralized, local media. Some observers would consider this a step toward the NWICO goal. There has been a great increase in local radio in Europe, and there is the beginning of community radio in Africa (in Kenya, for example). In countries where there is a tradition of local broadcasting, it tends to become more diversified and more responsive to local needs. In Africa and India there is some development of the rural press. Popular theater and various forms of folk media are recognized as important forms of local media in developing countries.

The tendency toward decentralization provides the opportunity for greater response to local cultural and linguistic conditions. It may also strengthen an infrastructure of local organization and local government in a country. The development of forms of smaller, local media provides more access to lower-status groups and enables minorities or local organizations to have their own media.

Participatory Communication

Perhaps the central NWICO issue is the principle that the ordinary person has the right of at least indirect participation in the governance of the public media, much as the ordinary citizen has the right of political participation. This implies that all sectors of the population should have the opportunity to contribute to the pool of information that provides the basis for local or national decision-making. The public should also have access to the tools of media production and the technical help to make its own programming.

At present, policy and administration of public communication tend to be the preserve of a small professional elite or, in commercial systems, financial-advertising interests. It has been proposed that mechanisms be established for broad consensual decision-making and permanent coordinating councils representing all sectors of the population, including minorities and marginal groups. This would provide more systematic representation in questions of general media policy, the organization and management of decisions on program orientation, and evaluation of programming. A basic principle is that communication is an individual and social right and that society only delegates the execution of this right to professionals.

To ensure greater accountability to the public, the following kinds of steps are being discussed:
a) More representative media ownership structures, preferable beyond the simple dichotomy of private or state ownership.
b) Development of new concepts of public law governing information and communication systems and the legal definition of rights, such as the right to participate in the public communication process.
c) Forms of financing public communication that will protect it from minority monopoly interests.

It is generally recognized that more participatory communication structures can come about only if there is a parallel development of more participatory *political* institutions and a more equitable access to economic opportunities.

Education for Participatory Communication

Many argue that the kind of participatory communication suggested above will be possible only if a new kind of "media education" is an integral part of primary and secondary education. Schools should, first, prepare citizens to be more active and discriminating users of available information, especially in view of the flood of information coming with the advent of cable television, satellites, and computerized data bases.

Secondly, schools can prepare citizens to communicate actively in the public media not only at a local community level, but also at a regional and, through representative bodies, at a national level. The young should have production experience in a variety of media to demystify the media image and learn how media languages express reality. It is important that all citizens sense that they are creators of culture.

Thirdly, if the public is going to participate in the decision-making structure of the mass media, it must become cognizant of how this decision-making takes place. The public must also know how the ordinary citizen can have access to decision-making and other information about the functioning of local and national media.

All this implies that media professionals be educated to greater openness to participation of the public and that mechanisms be developed for the mutual cooperation of professionals and the public.

Questioning Authoritarian Models in the Science of Communication

When media studies first began to emerge as a field of scientific research, there was a fascination with the power of the media to cause effects in the attitudes and actions of users. Researchers were ready to put themselves at the service of media administrators who wanted to change attitudes and persuade the public to buy, vote—or accept Christ. In this period the classic model of source→channel→receiver→effects developed. Much of the early research was concerned with measuring in a quantifiable way just how many persons were affected and to what degree.

Gradually, researchers gave up the premise that a "source" had to have "effects." It became apparent that persons approach the media or any other source of information with personal questions and the simple desire to make sense out of their situation. They pick and choose from many sources of information as they construct their vision of the world and their values. In this search they are conditioned by their level of education, economic opportunities, historical contexts, and the like. In short, communication researchers are much more likely to see the process of communication starting not with a media source but with the person or groups who need and want particular types of information or entertainment. The focus is on how media users *construct* meaning, not simply how they *absorb* meaning. This implies more respect for personal freedom and dignity.

Researchers have also begun to question whether their role is simply to make mass media more effective or whether media can be reformed when the problem lies in undemocratic media structures. Many researchers feel that they can better fulfill their responsibility to the public by unmasking self-serving media ideologies and by systematically analyzing the concentration of social power and mechanisms of social control in the media.

HOW CAN CHRISTIAN COMMUNICATORS CONTRIBUTE TO NWICO?

The history of the major issues in the search for a new communication order describes a process toward long-term goals. It also describes processes that many Christian communicators can detect going on around them. Many may be inclined to say, "Yes, that is what I feel should be the goal" or "Yes, that is what we have been trying to do." Some may recognize that these issues are close to the heart of their own gospel values.

Some may feel, too, that the present pattern of communication in at least their part of the church is far from the goals of the new communication order. This was the experience afforded by a meeting of leaders of church work in communication in Latin America held in October 1982 in São Paulo, Brazil. They met to discuss the role of the church in developing the New World Information and Communication Order in the Latin American context.

The meeting opened with a discussion of the goals of more democratic communication in Latin America. As the church leaders saw its implications, they began to recognize that many of the problems of communication in society at large could be found in the church itself. The church is a microcosm of Latin American society and has absorbed many of its patterns of communication. By the second day of the meeting, a number of the religious communicators were suggesting that there should be a "mini-NWICO" within the church itself.

These admissions were coming from a Latin American church that was sufficiently aware of the problem to think of holding such a meeting. Nearly all the religious communicators present had been involved with some form of alternative communication: group communications, independent documentation centers, radio stations with innovative ways of direct participation in the programming, and other uses of media that serve the poor.

Most of those present were aware of how difficult it is to develop the kind of working models that would offer an alternative to communications controlled by powerful elites and supported by transnational interests. Many of the forms of alternative communication that the church has developed now appear obvious. But initially it was not obvious what might be done. The communication situation in Latin America is every bit as complex as in other regions of the world. It was a challenge to the Christian imagination to translate ideals into practice in the midst of poverty, repression, lack of technical support, and all the other problems of underdevelopment. But in many cases there developed something new and unique not only for the church but for Latin American society. Some persons had literally risked their lives to give this kind of living witness to Christian values in communication.

When the church approaches media professionals to suggest guidelines, these professionals have a perfect right to say, "Show me some practical working models of what you are talking about." It becomes obvious that the most impressive thing for media professionals is the living witness of Christians. And the church leaders meeting in São Paulo came to realize how far they were from realizing their own ideals and how much more work they have to do right at home in the church.

From the practical experience of many Christian communicators around the world, one can abstract some simple and obvious guidelines suggesting how Christians can help build a new communication order.

1. Search for a deeper awareness of the history of communication institutions in one's own country and how this has influenced the way we try to organize communication within the church.

2. Search also for an awareness of changes in communication taking place in one's country. By this is meant not just technological changes, but the questioning that is going on, media reform movements, innovative alternative experi-

ences. Some of these may seem impractical, but much of it may suggest the action of the Spirit in history. It may also help us to see more clearly how gospel values translate into the culture and society in which we live.

3. We need to question deeply, in the light of the gospel, the models of communication we are using. We must be convinced that media technology is never simply a neutral instrument to be used for the goals of Christianity. Technology usually brings with it a typical social structure of communication—for example, very vertical and authoritarian, or more interactive. Particular media already have a "language," typical genres of programming, and they are directed to groups of persons with particular needs.

4. Most importantly, we must be true to our own Christian instincts. If we sense a conflict between what we feel would be the best expression of our values and the models we are using, we must reflect on what changes might be needed. We need a deep awareness of our distinct Christian cultural identity within a secular technical society. If we are faithful to our inspirations, we may find ourselves gradually evolving a very innovative way of communication not only for giving witness to the gospel but also for contributing to the new communication order developing around us.

CHAPTER SEVEN

Communication and the Church in India

Gaston Roberge

The church is a society of men, women, young adults, and children. By its very nature, it is always engaged in various kinds of communication. Members of the church communicate among themselves, church leaders communicate with other members, and the church as a whole communicates with nonmembers. Communication, therefore, is not something accidental, optional, for the church: it is its very life. That is why a theologian has said, and rightly, "the church *is* communication."[1] Of course, the same can be said of all human societies. Any social group *is* communication. However, there is something special in the case of the church—namely, this staggering fact: the church communicates with God. The church endeavors to establish and foster communication between God and all men and women of the world.[2]

It is by fostering human-divine communication that the church facilitates communication and even communion among persons. But even as it makes its specific contribution, the church is not divorced from the larger human community. It is enriched and supported in its life by the progress of humankind. In the area of communications especially, the human community has passed through many far-reaching experiences. Reflection on those experiences is articulated in a large body of theory. This complex theory indicates two main concerns: the human development of all persons through communication processes, and the ever greater use of technology for ever more efficient communication. These two concerns are interrelated: the more potent the instruments of communication, the more reason there is for being concerned about the human community. For the very effectiveness of the new, gigantic communication media, such as television, entails not only a threat to, but even infringement of, human freedom.

The international community has expressed its concern in the very rich, humanistic, though nontheological Report of the MacBride Commission, *Many Voices, One World*.[3] However, the development of communication techniques—the technologization of communication—is not merely a matter of theory: it is a fact. And it is taking place at a speed that astonishes everyone. For instance, specialists long ago announced the eventual development of video technology in India. Nobody, however, had any idea of the speed at which that phenomenon would overtake us. In 1974 there was perhaps only one private institution in Calcutta that owned its own video tape recorder. As late as 1981, it was still felt by some planners that to set up a video center in Calcutta would be premature. Less than two years later, however, by mid-1983, Indians had already invested, according to one estimate, over 7 billion rupees (approx. U.S. $585 million) in the purchase of color VCRs and TV sets. It is believed that video can be found in as many as 400 cities and towns in India including very remote places.[4]

In 1984, "video coaches" circulate throughout the country, and in Ahmedabad women selling vegetables in the local market handle with remarkable ease and success U-matic video cameras: they have entered Martha Stuart's village video network.[5] One may still object to television and video in India, of course, but television might turn out to be the best medium for voicing one's argument.

This, then, is the context of my discussion of the Indian church and the communications media.[6] The church is witnessing at home and abroad, a rapid development in communication technology. It strives to catch up with these developments. It also wishes to celebrate the advances that promise so much good for humankind. But, on the other hand, the church discovers that the new technological advances embody ever more powerful forms of domination, inequality, exploitation, and dehumanization. The church is growing acutely aware that the social problems now experienced in communications are the contemporary form of age-old injustices. Will strengthening the mass media aggravate the contemporary experience of oppression and injustice?

Before exploring these questions, however, it might be useful to discuss the role of communication in the life of the church, and the relationship between evangelization and communication.

EVANGELIZATION, COMMUNICATION, DEVELOPMENT

The greatest obstacle met by the church in its communication ministry is a certain (mis)conception of evangelization. Communication is for communion. Healthy communication is democratic, emancipatory, essentially developmental. Evangelization, on the other hand, is sometimes conceived as purposeful and aggressive, aimed at winning converts. Evangelization thus practiced thwarts the process of communication and is nothing more than bad communication. Indeed, evangelization aiming at "giving the faith" to "pagans" is bad communication twice over. For faith is not a thing, and communication is never the transfer of a thing.

Faith is a personal relationship, and communication is the cultivation of personal relationships. Such evangelization as described above is bad evangelization, because the message of Christ is emancipatory. It bears fruit in communion, not in "winning." Furthermore, the "pagans" to whom it wants to "give the faith" are not necessarily "faithless"; at times they know and love Christ without belonging to the church.

Raimundo Panikkar sees the evolution of the self-consciousness of the church in five great periods of time or *kairos*. Panikkar's "kairology" comprises: witness (and martyrdom in the primitive church); a call for a change of mores (from the time of Constantine onward); crusade (facing the Muslim world); mission (from 1492 onward, facing uneuropeanized peoples); and dialogue.

It is striking that Panikkar's "kairology" parallels diverse ways in which the church communicates with the world. The present *kairos,* that of dialogue, is the time of communications par excellence. That is as it should be: the world with which the church interacts today is a world in which communication is given paramount importance. This world is a world of communication, this world *is* communication.

For many church persons, however, the world is still either a territory to conquer or a people to civilize in the name of Christ. The old instinct of the crusader or the zeal of the missionary, characteristic of a past *kairos,* are still at work in the heart of the church. As a result, communication is not seen as a locus of dialogue. On the contrary, some ecclesiastics still claim "as a birthright the use and possession of all instruments . . . necessary or useful for the formation of Christians and for every activity undertaken on behalf of man's salvation."[7]

It is not my point here that the crusade charism or the mission charism should be repressed within the church. Panikkar's "kairology" is not a "chronology" in which one period of time succeeds another. The various *kairos* moments are phases in which one particular aspect of the functioning of the church is evoked by its historical context, but not to the exclusion of other forms of *kairos*. There was dialogue in the primitive church, for instance, and other communication forms are not extinct in the *kairos* of dialogue.

Even within a pluralist view of church activity, it seems to me that the church today gives too much importance to "conversion" as a change from one "religion" to another. Although the Bible relentlessly asks for a conversion of heart, the church demands membership in its community.

Missionaries have at times failed to notice that if St. Francis Xavier longed, according to the theology of his time, to "convert" the whole world to Christ, St. Thérèse of Lisieux never used the word "conversion" in her writings, except to describe her own spiritual evolution, which was one of communion with Christ, and except in the single case of a notorious Christian "sinner," Pranzini.

When referring to her missionary vocation and to that of two priests entrusted to her spiritual care, St. Thérèse spoke of "making Christ known and loved."

To make a person known and loved is a delicate endeavor. Propaganda, persuasive discourses, and arguments are rarely the best ways to achieve that purpose. How far can one go, how "aggressive" can one be, in making Christ "known and loved"? That is largely determined by circumstances, and above all by Christ's inspiration at every moment. Communication in evangelization is tripartite, involving the evangelized, the evangelizer, and Christ. Eventually the evangelizer gives way to Christ, and communication takes place between the evangelized person and Christ.

I shall never finish pondering the infinite gentleness of God's ways. After all, it was Christ—not I the evangelizer—who died on a cross for the evangelized. In making Christ known and loved, I should not be more intrusive than Christ himself. Secondly, the relationship of the evangelized with Christ should be emancipatory—indeed, developmental. If it is not, then the evangelized has not received Christ, the savior. The evangelized has only been enslaved to a sham Christ, a creation of human lust for power.

If evangelization is sometimes bad communication, development communication is often bad communication. Development implies change. Something must change if something else is to develop; something must die in order that something new may be born. This process may be mysterious but, as such, it is not problematic. What may constitute a problem is the freedom or coercion with which the process is brought about.

A comparison may prove useful here. I may be vastly enriched if I learn a foreign language of my own free will. This new ability to communicate may prove very emancipatory. On the other hand, if a foreign language is forced upon me, even though in the end I do learn it—which is a gain—the new language, nonetheless, is for me a form of bondage and a cultural impoverishment. However, even when I learn a language of my own free will and however enriched I find myself as a result of learning that language, I am nonetheless impoverished to the extent that meanwhile I have not cultivated my mother tongue. That impoverishment is not destructive of my identity though, because I have willed it. Besides, the impoverishment is largely offset by the gain.

In the implementation of cultural and linguistic policies, the questions arise: Who has the right to decide on these issues? How can we ensure that a decision affecting a group will be taken collectively? It may be that in a particular case it is advisable that a person or a community relinquish their mother tongue and adopt another language. But only the persons involved in this transaction can freely make such a decision.

Yet, there must be some form of "intrusion" into the lives of others, whether for development or evangelization. One must take the risk—and the attendant responsibility—of one's interventions. If that were not the case, then we would all be condemned to live in splendid isolation. Indeed, there would be no possibility of communication, let alone of love. The risks, of course, are great.

Ethnocentrism, a belief in one's cultural superiority, is the pitfall of development work. Pride, a belief in one's own righteousness, is the pitfall of evangelization.

Inasmuch as both the development worker and the evangelizer are proclaiming the kingdom of God—the former heralding and working out its advent and the latter pointing to its presence—it is likely that they can help each other in their respective tasks. Both have to respect the personal freedom inherent in human nature. Both have to lay aside mechanistic views of communication. Both have to create holistic visions where the development and salvation of every human being is seen in terms of an ever growing integration into an overall design—a design that, for the Christian, is personalized in Christ.

THE NEED FOR HEALTHY THEORY

We need a vision, a theory. (The English word "theory" comes from the Greek *theorein,* "to look at and see." When you have a theory, you know where you are going.) It should be evident that we need ongoing theological reflection—"looking at and seeing," theorizing—on church communication. Although efforts have been made to equip the church with communication instruments, commensurate efforts have not been made to create the required conceptual tools.

One of the leading theological journals of the Indian Catholic Church, *Vidyajyoti,* dedicated its September 1983 issue to the topic of communications. There was not even one article by a theologian in it. Of course, that collection of articles should not be taken as the definitive expression of the reflection of the Indian Church on the subject of communication. It is striking, all the same, that the editor of the journal did not think it necessary to have any Indian theologian write an article on communication.

When I read works in theology, I often feel that their authors' theory of communication is poor. And when I write on communication from a theological angle, I am aware that my theology may be inadequate. In particular, it may be that I do not adequately express theological difficulties regarding the various aspects of the communication ministry and communicational difficulties regarding the notion of evangelization. I think I have no reason to be ashamed of any such inadequacies: I am not a professional theologian. On the other hand, theologians should not feel embarrassed if they have not mastered the latest communication theories. What is a matter of shame, however, is that we—communicators, theologians, and philosophers—have not yet been able to discuss these matters in depth. It should be evident that a theological theory of communication can result only from a collaborative, interdisciplinary endeavor.

Throughout, I am using the phrase "communication theory" to mean first of all a theory of communication properly speaking, as well as a theory of information, of systems, of language and signs. Communication is a subject so encompassing that there is hardly any issue dealt with in philosophy or theology that does not imply in important ways a theory of communication in one or more of its aspects or components. I see no indication in the church in India that the required interdisciplinary study will be done in the near future.

Communicators have attempted to design communication courses for students in seminaries. I think that was a false approach. There is something amiss in having the subject of communication dealt with from outside philosophy or theology by visiting lecturers. Philosophy and theology professors should deal with the subject of communication. A philosophy or theology worthy of the name should deal with communication, and adequately. If it does not, then classes on communication theory can never fill in this lacuna. Communicators should be called upon only for training in the skills and techniques of communication.

I have tried a number of times to teach "communication" to seminarians and scholastics. I found that philosophy and theology students tend to become unteachable as they approach the end of their training, because of a premature closure of their interests in specific pastoral fields. In order to teach them some communication skills, I need to probe into their basic approach to communication. For these young persons have already absorbed, along with doctrinal principles and spiritual attitudes, a very rigid model of communication that makes it almost impossible for them to understand—let alone respond to—the communication theory and practice I can offer them. The communication model that has been in their minds informs their homiletics, their sacramental practice, their catechetics, their rapport with their flock and with persons outside the church. They think of themselves as the depositories of an ensemble of objective truths that they must simply transmit to others in its integrity.

Hence, their proclamation is a one-way process of the revelation of impersonal truth. Their sacramental life is *abstract* and *literary* because the signs and symbols in it are given as little importance as possible. But, on the contrary, should not the proclamation of the gospel be a personal challenge, a summons to personal commitment? Should not the practice of the sacraments be rooted in *concrete* signs in order to have significance at all levels of the person, conscious and subconscious? Finally, should not every effort be made to ensure that communication within the church be dialogical and democratic, even though the structure of the church is theocratic?

In my opinion the most urgent task awaiting the Indian church is a definition of the communication model inherent in the practice of the church and above all in the various treatises on philosophy and theology taught to future pastors. A courageous recognition of that model would make it possible to criticize it and then proceed to improve upon it. Unless this is done, any acquisition of skills or techniques will only promote unhealthy communication in the church.

THE INDIAN CHURCH AND NWICO

The involvement of the church in communications must have concrete forms, yet it cannot be measured solely in terms of the number of communication centers the church is running. We can also ask about the less tangible, less spectacular, achievements of the church in matters of communication. Where are our prominent communicators? Among our pastors—the most numerous recipients of specialized training—where are the scholars? Is there any Indian priest capable of giving a course in the philosophy or theology of communication? How many Christian film scholars could sit on a board of film censorship? Write serious criticism? Lecture on the art of film-making in secular universities? It is heartening to see that we have a few priests who can perform these services. It is disheartening to find that we have so few.

In spite of the pioneering work done here and there in India, the church has done little to use the new media of communication for its own benefit, and it has hardly contributed anything to the secular media—that is, to society at large. Our primary effort has been to equip ourselves with a few sound-recording studios and projectors for films and slides. The current video invasion will undoubtedly cause us to invest, rightly or wrongly, still more of our limited and shrinking resources in the purchase of equipment.

There is a gap between what the church says on communication and the practical attention it gives to communication. Around the time of the Second Vatican Council, the Catholic Church had grown aware of the importance of communication. But it seems that it could not sense the reason for that importance, because by and large it was still under the sway of its old, closed, self-consciousness as a missionary body, as the light of the nations and as the "universal sacrament of salvation" (Christ, of course, is the *lumen gentium*). Thus, instead of welcoming the media of communication as aids for dialogue, it first saw them as competitors. Failing to outwit them, it then sought to appropriate them for crusading or evangelizing. That is why the fundamental issues raised by the NWICO debate leaves the church somewhat indifferent. A church concerned primarily with church affairs can perceive such issues only as mundane and secular matters.

Two general conclusions can be deduced from the MacBride Report studied in the light of ecclesiastical documents on communication:

1) In order that it may contribute to the creation of a New World Information and Communication Order, the church will have to face and solve the problem of its own autocratic communication.
2) The church could utilize the MacBride Report as a guide for its own involvement in the task of creating a New World Information and Communication Order.

The practical issues raised by church documents and the MacBride Report are so vast that I cannot hope to offer a satisfactory overall discussion of them in the limited framework of this paper. I shall instead deal with the question from a subjective point of view, drawing from my own experience, which, though limited, may be instructive and symptomatic of a number of attitudes impairing the work of the church and distracting attention from needs that call for action.

THE NEED FOR PRAGMATIC RESEARCH

When I came back from Hollywood trained as a film-maker, I was asked by fellow priests if I planned to make a film on Christ. In time the queries became more modest: was I to make gospel slides? There are here two complementary issues, each of which might call for lengthy comments. Of necessity I shall limit myself to what seems more pertinent to NWICO.

The production of a film on Christ is perhaps one of the most problematic projects conceivable. In order to make a commercially viable film one would have to offer a rehash of all the cliché images of Christ that popular Christian iconography has created. Although the Holy Spirit may prompt a person to love Christ through very deficient images (is not the church itself just such an image?), one can wonder whether such a project is wise from a point of view central to the MacBride Report, that of indigenous cultures.

Secondly, a religious film is one of the most difficult sort of films to make and requires a great esthetic sensitivity, which is not the hallmark of the film industry anywhere in the world. Film-makers of great stature can—as Pier Paolo Pasolini has shown—make significant films on Christ. But these films do not always meet market demands and, above all, they cannot be "made to order." And when church persons ask for films on Christ, they rarely have that sort of film in mind. They rather think of films like *The Robe* or *King of Kings*, which are not religious films.

The production of slides to illustrate gospel scenes raises a still more difficult cultural problem (though on a lower financial scale)—the problem of codes of representation. Each cultural area has its own manner of perception as well as of representation of time and space. One would not know how to represent gospel scenes for a specific group unless one studied the way the members of that group perceive time and space and the way in which they translate their perception. The only ones who would know these perfectly are, of course, the persons belonging to that milieu. However, the demands of mass production would gloss over such issues, attaching little importance to them because mass production of necessity ignores the cultural differences between groups. In the end the conclusion would easily be that, because slides made abroad are inexpensive and readily available, they are, after all, most appropriate.

There is, however, another solution to this problem: it consists in making it possible for "target" groups to make their own slides. With this aim in mind, the Chitrabani training center in Calcutta designed a rudimentary magic lantern, inviting users to make the slides they needed. One hundred lanterns have been manufactured. They are used mainly by development organizations; most pastoral centers prefer more sophisticated equipment and ready-made slides!

I am well aware that as I develop this argument some of the very persons for whom the magic lantern was designed are already roaming around with video cameras! The rapid spread of advanced technology in India is yet another issue, and I shall address it later on in this paper. My concern here is technology design respectful of the manner of perception and representation of particular groups of persons.

The production of films, slides, and posters is made more problematic by a yet larger question, that of symbols. This area is beginning to receive attention from Indian Christian theologians.[8] Much more research is required, on a much larger scale, given the numerous cultural groups of India. From a purely pragmatic point of view, the need for research in communication is felt with regard to even the smallest audiovisual production.

THE NEED FOR PROFESSIONALISM

Professionals have the reputation of being expensive. And so they are. As a result few church persons "dare" to approach them for the services they need. If the professional happens to be a priest, it is assumed that his services will be much less expensive. That is often the case, yet the services are still deemed too expensive, because church persons approaching a professional communicator generally underestimate the value of the services they ask for. The pastor asking for a service believes he is overcharged and is indignant; the priest rendering the service believes he is underestimated and is offended.

In fact, few professionals are as cost-conscious as professional communicators. Pastors and school headmasters have a tendency to think that what is inexpensive is economical. Professional communicators see things differently. They are used to working with larger sums of money. But they assess their expenses in terms of the number of persons benefited by these expenses. For instance, a snapshot such as a pastor might wish to have as a souvenir of a function may be deemed an extravagant expenditure by a professional because, however little it costs, it is useful to only a small number of persons and often for only a short time. An audiovisual production professionally executed will be much more expensive, but it will be deemed economical by the communicator because it has enduring value to a large number of persons.

The ultimate authority over church-related communication centers is usually vested in a group of church persons comprising both professional communicators and persons who are not from the field of communication. Because of their different perceptions of budgetary matters, they are sure to have different views on financial issues. Threshing out these differences uses up so much time and energy that other policy matters, in many ways more significant, are neglected. But the issue of money, surprisingly important to persons dedicated to religious poverty or to simplicity of life, is concrete enough for all to feel competent to handle it. However, not all are competent to do so. Although nonprofessional decision-makers have important contributions to make regarding the policies of a communication center—Whom should it serve? Should it be a catechetical or an educational center?—they usually are ill-prepared to deal with budgetary matters.

Church leaders have acquired expertise in the management of schools. But the management of a communication center has little in common with that of a school. The management must be much more "nervous" and responsive to evolving situations. The scale of salaries and conditions of work of communicators do not compare with those of teachers. And, finally, the budget of even the smallest center may seem huge to a nonprofessional person.

THE NEED FOR CONCERN FOR COMMUNICATION ISSUES

The church is in earnest when it is attacked or when it feels threatened as a minority institution. It is more difficult for the church to feel involved in communication issues that do not touch it directly but nonetheless affect the quality of life of millions of persons. For instance, if the church had an understanding of the profound influence of the mass media on the people, it might have introduced classes on this subject in its numerous educational institutions. The Jesuits, to single out a particular group of educators, run nearly one hundred high schools in India. Media education, a primary need today, is not yet offered in those schools. Nor is there any effort made to educate adults on communication issues in parishes and in informal educational groups conducted by the church.

Although the church is aware of the large place communications occupy in our lives, it does not seem to have grasped the fact that as a result, nothing less than a new society is emerging. The church has not yet found—has not yet been motivated to look for—suitable modes of action to translate its awareness into a commitment. It is not sufficient for the church to just wait and see.

The world is changing. The MacBride Report was not a terminal point, but an important moment in an ongoing process. In late 1983 the Director General of UNESCO had this to say:

> The new world information and communication order has now acquired legitimacy, in the world community (. . .) the process in question is evolving and is irreversible. A new world information and communication order will emerge, whether we like it or not, as a result of two things from which there can be no escape. On the one hand, we have the technological revolution now under way, which will soon usher in radically new forms of communication both in the industrialized and in the developing countries. On the other hand, we find throughout the world and in many different social groups a strong desire for broader and more equitable participation in the various currents of communication, whose role both in the development of societies and in the lives of individuals is increasingly clearly recognized. The need to reduce the imbalances observable in this area, including not only those affecting North and South but also those found within each group of countries and within single countries, is keenly felt today by an ever-increasing number of population groups.[9]

THE NEED TO CLARIFY THE ATTITUDE OF THE CHURCH TOWARD COMMUNICATION TECHNOLOGY

The physical world is ambivalent, indeed multivalent. It all depends on what humankind does with it. For, although humankind is only part of the world, it alone has the power of interfering with the natural evolution of the world.

Communication technology has today been given great importance in human life. Anything that is important to humankind should be significant to the church. But communication technology is a difficult object to assess. It is at once a way of life, a manner of knowing and feeling, a network of institutions, and a mammoth complexus of instrumentation.

If the church saw it as its primary function to help persons grow precisely as persons, it might be easier for it to approach communication technology with compassion and with hope in the power of the Risen Lord. The world awaits the salvific action of Christ. Communication media, meanwhile, are used to keep populations in subservience, produce psychic pollution, undermine the very fabric of language by publicity campaigns and control information in the service of dominative powers. Communication essentially meant for communion is used to divide persons and peoples by malign propaganda.

By the same token, communication media enlarge the field of knowledge and open it to all human beings. The media can unify and integrate our "global village." The media have reestablished a more healthy balance in our perception of reality. They have given more importance to imagination and intuition after centuries of rationalism. There is so much that is evil and so much that is good!

This is a time when the church can contribute immensely to the spiritual welfare of all humankind. But it will be able to make its contribution only if it is prepared to serve. In practice, however, it seems that the church is not interested in the mass media. The main reason for this is that it cannot control these media, or use them for crusade and mission. As a result the contribution of the church to—indeed, the salvific presence of the church in—the mass media is nil.

Apart from the mass media, there are many other communication instruments—photographs, pictures, slides, films, video tapes. These the church can own and control—and one witnesses a fervor that smacks of technological messianism! Although it is one of my responsibilities as a priest communicator to foster the use of audiovisual aids in the service of the church, I often find myself discouraging such use. For instance, I discourage use of audiovisual aids when I find that they would only strengthen nondialogical, nonparticipatory, nonemancipatory, nondemocratic, in a word, unhealthy—communication. It should be clear that only healthy communication is suitable for proclaiming Christ's liberating message.

Another of my concerns is the exclusive use by the church of its instruments of communication. In a country where so many persons are deprived of essential commodities, it is scandalous for the church to own and use expensive communication instruments exclusively for its own members, or exclusively for enlarging the size of its membership. Moreover, although we should put at the service of the word of God the best means available, we should see to it that these means are consonant with the simplicity of the message we want to convey and are not offensive to the simplicity of the persons to whom the message is to be conveyed. These principles are easy to enunciate, but their application is not easy. I believe that sincerity, tolerance, and dialogue will permit us to set our courage in the best direction and adjust it as we go along.

Earlier I acknowledged that although I am engaging in theological theorizing, I am not a professional theologian. As I conclude this discussion, a similar acknowledgment has to be made regarding pastoral ministries understood in the parochial sense of "formation of Christians." I myself do not have extensive experience in such work and, thus, I may not be as sensitive as I should be to the needs experienced by priests engaged in parish work.

Is my perception of the Indian church and communication too negative? Are there only defects and lacunae to be observed? Surely not. However interested as I am in the *healthy* theory and practice of communication in the church, my attention is drawn to communication deficiencies with an almost clinical relentlessness. But I do not simply decry these deficiencies. I wish rather to contribute toward healing them. I am also conscious of my own limitations. Yet I rely neither on my own strength nor even on that of the church. My hope is in the Risen Lord.

NOTES

1. Avery Dulles, *The Church Is Communication* (address prepared for the Bishop's Communications Institute, Loyola University, New Orleans, 1971), Rome, Multimedia International Publications, 1982.

2. Communication between human beings is fraught with problems—linguistic, philosophical, and ethical. We can expect, then, that communication between human beings and God will give rise to very special problems indeed.

3. *Many Voices, One World: Report by the International Commission for the Study of Communication Problems,* London/New York/Paris, Kogan Page/Unipub/ UNESCO, 1980.

4. See *India Today,* June 30, 1983, p. 60.

5. "Martha: Barefoot, Pregnant, and behind the Plough," *Development Forum* (United Nations), vol. 11, no. 4, May 1983.

6. The Indian church has been involved in communication for many years, first through publishing books, magazines, and newspapers—especially in Kerala and Tamil Nadu—and more recently through other traditional and modern media. In 1966 the National Commission for Social Communications was founded.

The *Christian Communication Directory of Asia* (Munich, 1982) discloses the following data: The Catholic Church runs 137 presses in India. Of these, 66 are in Kerala, 22 in Tamil Nadu, and 49 in the rest of the nation. Catholic periodicals number over 300. It is striking that many of the bigger presses were started before the 1960s. There have been important newcomers after 1966, such as the Gujarat Sahitya Prakash publishing house (1979) and the periodical *Fatima* (1973), with a circulation of 36,500 in 1979. The overall impression, however, is that there has been no significant thrust of the church in the press medium since Vatican II. If we look at other media, the picture is both heartening and disheartening. We can be proud indeed to have media centers such as Amruthavani (Secunderabad), Santhome (Madras), Kalai Kaviri (Trichy), the Xavier Institute of Communications (Bombay), the Canara Communication Center, the Tuticorin Pastoral Centre, and the Chitrabani training center (Calcutta). These seven centers employ some 147 persons. There are some 20 other very small media centers in India, employing some 22 additional persons.

7. *Inter Mirifica,* no. 3.

8. See M. Amaladoss, *Do Sacraments Change? Variable and Invariable Elements in Sacramental Rites,* Bangalore, Theological Publications in India, 1979.

9. *The Month at UNESCO,* 111 (Oct./Nov. 1983) 28.

CHAPTER EIGHT

Select Annotated Bibliography on a New World Information and Communication Order (NWICO)

Colleen Roach

BOOKS AND PAMPHLETS ON NWICO

AHCENE, DJABALLAH, BELKACEM. *Aspects du nouvel ordre international de l'information.* Algiers, Office des Publications Universitaires, 1980, 217 pp. Chronicles nonaligned/UNESCO role in promoting NWICO. Includes case study of the Algerian experience of the "decolonization of information."

ARRIETA, MARIO. *Obstáculos para un nuevo orden informativo internacional.* Mexico City, Editorial Nueva Imagen, 1980, 415 pp. Critical study of the existing order, examined on the basis of work of the Trilateral Commission and the concept of "technetronic era." Proposes alternative strategy for developing countries.

AYAR, FARID. *Preliminary Ideas on the Foundations for the New International Information Order.* Beirut, Federation of Arab News Agencies, 1978, 18 pp. Advocates information exchange between European and Arab news agencies as an essential step toward NWICO. Also provides information on the Federation of Arab News Agencies.

For an earlier version of this bibliography, see Colleen Roach, *Media Development*, London, January 1980.

BECKER, JÖRG. *Africa on the Way to a New International Information Order.* Geneva, Institute Universitaire d'Etudes du Développement, 1980, 50 pp. Deals with racism in Western media, Western penetration of African media, and contours of NWICO in Africa. Concludes with provocative question: "Could it not be that African models constitute a reasonable media offer for Europeans?"

BECKER, JÖRG. ed. *Free Flow of Information: Informationen zur Neuen Internationalen Informationsordnung.* Frankfurt/Main, Gemeinschaftswerk der Evangelischen Publizistik, 1979, 318 pp. Articles on NWICO, divided into three sections: (1) the structure of the international flow of information; (2) a case study: Chile; (3) documents on NWICO.

BOURGES, HERVÉ. *Décoloniser l'information.* Paris, Editions Cana, 1978, 160 pp. Introduction to Third World demands concerning news flow. The author draws on his own experience in North Africa to present the case for "decolonization of information."

BULATOVIC, VLADISLAVA. *Non-Alignment and Information.* Belgrade, Federal Committee for Information/Jugoslovenska Stvarnost, 1978, 120 pp. A summary of nonaligned activities in the field of information. Also answers Western attacks on the nonaligned news pool.

CAMPBELL, FRANK. *The New International Information and Communication Order: A Caribbean Perspective.* Georgetown, Guyana, Ministry of Information, 1980, 27 pp. Comments on "old information order" and what must be done by Caribbean governments to promote NWICO.

GONZALEZ MANET, ENRIQUE. *Descolonización de la información.* Prague, International Organization of Journalists, 1979, 124 pp. A study of communication technology as a structural component of the Western economic system. Provides a critical analysis of Western research and the new strategy for NWICO.

GUNTER, JOHNATHAN. *The United States and the Debate on the World "Information Order."* Washington, D.C., Academy for Educational Development, 1978, 172 pp. A document prepared for U.S. policy formulation on NWICO. The issue is broken down into four basic areas: news flow, mass culture, technology transfer, and national sovereignty vis-à-vis communication rights.

HAMELINK, CEES. *Towards a New World Information Order.* Geneva, World Council of Churches, 1978, 22 pp. + appendices. Overview of basic aspects of NWICO, including implementation agenda for churches.

HAMMARBERG, THOMAS. *New Information Order: Balance and Freedom.* Stockholm, Ministry of Education and Cultural Affairs, 1978. The underlying assumption behind this work is that there is no conflict between a "free" and "balanced" flow of information. Examines Western news agencies, the nonaligned pool, and national communication structures.

HARRIS, PHIL. *Putting the NIIO into Practice: The Role of Inter Press Service.* Rome, IPS Research and Information Office, 1979, 14 pp. Proposals on the contribution of an alternative Third World news agency toward establishing NWICO.

INTERNATIONAL ORGANIZATION OF JOURNALISTS. *Reflections around UNESCO.* (Presented by Kaarle Nordenstreng). Prague, IOJ, 1978, 69 pp. Summary of IOJ speeches and documents dealing with UNESCO information activities.

KOLOSSOV, Y. and TSEPOV, B. *The New International Information Order and the Problem of Maintaining Peace.* Moscow, Editions Naouka, 1984, 72 pp. The authors, specialists in international law, examine the Soviet position on a wide range of questions, including international cooperation within the framework of the UN and UNESCO. Considerable attention is devoted to U.S.S.R. efforts to have mass information regulated under international law.

KROLOFF, GEORGE, and COHEN, SCOTT. *The New World Information Order.* Washington, D.C., United States Senate, Committee on Foreign Relations, 1977, 38 pp. An official view of what the United States stands to lose and gain with NWICO. Predicts that informatics will be the single most important issue in international communication debates.

LEGUM, COLIN, and CORNWELL, J. *A Free and Balanced Flow.* Lexington, Mass., Lexington Books, 1978, 77 pp. Report of the Twentieth Century Fund Task Force on the International Flow of News. The authors conclude that the present situation is "an inevitable consequence of historical and technological developments."

LOPEZ-ESCOBAR, ESTEBAN. *Análisis del "nuevo orden" internacional de la información.* Pamplona, Ediciones Universidad de Navarra, 1978, 484 pp. Overview of the call for NWICO, emphasizing international news structures, news agencies, and the "free flow of information" concept.

MANKEKAR, DINKER RAO. *One-way News Flow: Neo-Colonialism via News Media.* Delhi, Clarion Books, 1978, 169 pp. An evaluation of Third World charges against the quality and content of Western news. Third World struggles in the area of information are also outlined.

———. *Whose Freedom? Whose Order?* Delhi, Clarion Books, 1981, 224 pp. Plea by one of the leading Third World advocates of NWICO. Argues that it is in the interest of the Western world to promote goals of a new order.

MILLÁN, FATIMA. *Nuevo orden económico y nuevo orden informativo internacional: análisis de una semana en la prensa de América Latina.* Mexico City, Instituto Latinoamericano de Estudios Transnacionales (ILET), 1980, 90 pp. Content analysis of Latin American treatment of development issues, based on coverage of the fourth ministerial meeting of the Group of 77.

NASCIMIENTO, CHRISTOPHER. *The World Communication Environment.* Georgetown, Guyana, Ministry of Information, 1981, 67 pp. A collection of speeches of the Guyanan information minister, touching upon the issues related to the NWICO debate: the North American coverage of the Jonestown tragedy; the introduction of television into developing nations; communication as a development-support tool; allocation of world resources.

NORDENSTRENG, KAARLE. *The Mass Media Declaration of UNESCO.* Norwood, N.J., Ablex, 1984, 384 pp. First comprehensive book on what has been referred to as the "Declaration on a New World Information/ Communication Order." Includes extensive documentation on the UNESCO/Non-Aligned activities.

PAVLIC, BREDA, and HAMELINK, CEES. *The New International Economic Order: Links Between Economics and Communications.* Paris, UNESCO (fourth-coming). Deals with relationship between the New International Economic Order and NWICO. Main focus is on problems of developing countries.

REYES MATTA, FERNANDO, ed. *La información en el nuevo orden internacional.* Mexico City, ILET, 1977, 260 pp. Texts by well-known specialists on the following subjects: international information and the transnational structure; international news agencies; technology and global communication; perspectives for change.

RIGHTER, ROSEMARY. *Whose News? Politics, the Press and the Third World.* London, André Deutsch, 1978, 272 pp. A study on the dangers of NWICO or freedom of the press and human rights. Focuses particular attention on UNESCO advocacy of national communication policies.

ROBINSON, GERTRUDE JOCH, ed. *Assessing the New World Information Order Debate: Evidence and Proposals.* United States International Communications Division, Association for Education in Journalism, 1982, 134 pp. Articles treating the following themes: UNESCO debates; media imperialism theory; foreign correspondents and development news.

SALINAS, RAQUEL. *Communication Policies: A Crucial Issue for the Accomplishment of the New Information Order. The Case of Latin America.* Stockholm, Institute of Latin American Studies, 1978, 39 pp. An analysis of international developments that sustain the present search for NWICO. Emphasis is on national communication policies in Latin America.

Secretariat of State [Tunisia] for Information. *The New World Order for Information.* Tunis, 1977, 53 pp. Presentation of the basic elements involved in NWICO by spokesmen for one of the "front-line" countries. Accent on nonaligned information activities.

SOMAVÍA, JUAN. *Participación del tercer mundo en la comunicación internacional: Perspectivas despues de Nairobi.* Mexico City, ILET, 1978, 45 pp. Summary of major events up to and including the UNESCO General Conference in 1976. Advances conceptual and practical propositions for Third World participation in international communications.

SUSSMAN, LEONARD. *Warning of a Bloodless Dialect: Glossary for International Communications.* Washington, D.C., The Media Institute, 1983, 56 pp. An essay/glossary on resolutions, topics, and issues related to the NWICO debate. Terms such as "commercialization of the media," "media access," and the "right to communicate" are presented with definitions of the First World, the Second World (Marxist), the Third World, and UNESCO.

UNESCO. *Historical Background of the Mass Media Declaration* (New Communication Order Series, no. 9). Paris, 1979, 279 pp. Provides a brief history of the UNESCO Declaration on the Mass Media, as well as numerous annexes presenting various versions of the declaration, related resolutions, meetings and statements made by member states of the organization.

———. *Many Voices, One World.* Final Report of the International Commission for the Study of Communication Problems (MacBride Commission). London/New York/Paris, Kogan Page/Unipub/UNESCO, 1980, 312 pp. Study, by experts from 16 countries, of the "totality of communication problems in modern societies." One of the most complete analyses available of various aspects of the international communication debates.

VARIS, TAPIO; SALINAS, RAQUEL; and JOKELIN, RENNY. *International News and the New Information Order.* Tampere, University of Tampere, Institute of Journalism and Mass Communication, 1977, 149 pp. Each author treats a specific aspect of news in reference to the call for NWICO: European broadcasting; news agencies; a case study of Inter Press Service.

WORLD PRESS FREEDOM COMMITTEE. *The Media Crisis. . . .* Florida, 1980, 113pp. Collection of articles primarily by authors who oppose NWICO. Most texts center on the "state-control" argument.

———. *The Media Crisis . . . A Continuing Challenge.* Washington, D.C., 1982, 151 pp. Update of the 1980 work. Informative survey of various aspects of Western positions on international communication issues.

BOOKS AND PAMPHLETS ON RELATED ASPECTS OF NWICO

ARGUMEDO, ALCIRA. *Comunicación y democracia: una perspectiva tercermundista.* Mexico City, ILET, 1981, 22 pp. Analysis of the relationship between social communication and democracy, within the context of NWICO debates.

ARRIAGA, PATRICIA. *Publicidad, economía y comunicación masiva* (México-Estados Unidos). Sacramento, Mexico, Centro de Estudios Económicos y Sociales del Tercer Mundo (CEESTEM), Editorial Nueva Imagen, 1980, 324 pp. Offers critical perspective from the developing world on advertising, economics, and the mass media, with particular reference to Mexico and the United States. Also presents critique of dominant "cultural imperialism" model.

ATWOOD, L. ERWIN; BULLION, STUART, J.; and MURPHY, SHARON M. *International Perspectives on News.* Carbondale, Southern Illinois University Press, 1982, 201 pp. Papers of 15 media scholars participating at a symposium held at Southern Illinois University. Major topics include: communication and development; global news flow; assessment of U.S. media performance.

BARROS LEMEZ, ALVARO. *La televisión en América Latina.* Caracas, Instituto de Investigaciones de la Comunicación (ININCO), 1977, 37 pp. An analysis of the history and development of television in Latin America and its relationship to the transnational media industries.

BARTON, FRANK. *The Press of Africa: Persecution and Perseverance.* London,

Macmillan, 1979, 304 pp. Comprehensive view of the history and present state of the press in Africa. Treats three subjects: freedom of the press, the rural press; the profession of journalism in Africa.

BIELENSTEIN, DIETER. *Africa—Only a Crisis for the German Media? Problems of Reporting Africa.* Bonn, Institut für Internationale Begegnungen, 1976, 15 pp. A report on the findings of a series of discussions on the quality and quantity of media reporting on Africa in West Germany. The report concludes that "crisis reporting" of Africa predominates.

BOYD-BARRET, OLIVER. *The International News Agencies.* Beverly Hills, Calif., Sage Publications, 1980, 284 pp. Examines the "big four" news agencies. Discusses history of each agency, revenues, and the effects of new technology. Also touches upon the question of whether or not national news agencies in the Third World are able to compete with the "big four."

———, and PALMER, MICHAEL. *Le trafic des nouvelles: les agences mondiales d'information.* Paris, Editions Alain Moreau, 1981, 712 pp. One of the most thoroughly documented studies available on Western news agencies. Includes critical analysis of the history of each agency, its financial sources, and the way operations are affected by new technology. Also examines Third World news agencies within the context of the NWICO debates.

CANTOR HAGNANI, JOSÉ, and MURARO, HERIBERTO. *Las empresas multinacionales en el proceso de produción y circulación de material filmico en Argentina.* Buenos Aires, Facultad Latinoamericana de Ciencias Sociales (FLACSO), 1976, 134 pp. A well-documented study of the presence of multinationals in the Argentine film industry, the forms through which they exercise their influence, and the effects on local production.

CHEVALDONNÉ, FRANCIS. *La communication inégale.* Paris, CNRS, 1981. A study of the consumption of cultural merchandise in Algeria. In examining the socio-economic conditions of audience reception, the author focuses on a much-neglected aspect of the NWICO debates.

COMPAINE, BENJAMIN, ed. *Who Owns the Media? Concentration of Ownership in the Mass Communication Industry.* New York, Crown Publishers, 1979, 330 pp. A comprehensive study of ownership trends in the major American communication media. Provides a wealth of statistics on media concentration.

DACOSTA, ALCINO LUIS; ABOUBAKR; YEHIA; CHOPRA; PRAN; and REYES MATTA, FERNANDO. *News Values and Principles of Cross-Cultural Communication* (Reports and Papers on Mass Communication, no. 85). Paris, UNESCO, 1979, 52 pp. Divided into four sections: criteria for news selection in Africa; international news exchange in the Arab states; Asian news values; the concept of news in Latin America.

DIZARD, WILSON P., *The Coming Information Age.* New York, Longman, 1982, 213 pp. Discusses the specific technical, economic, and political realities involved in the shift to the "information age" in advanced industrial societies.

DORFMAN, ARIEL, and MATTELART, ARMAND. *How To Read Donald Duck:*

Imperialist Ideology in the Disney Comic. New York/Bagnolet, France, International General, 1975, 112 pp. An analysis of the ideology of the Disney comics, made at the time of the Popular Unity government in Chile; includes select bibliography.

ESTEINOU MADRID, JAVIER. *Los medios de comunicación y la construcción de la hegemonia.* Paris, Editorial Nueva Imagen, 1983. A theoretical analysis of the role of television in the reproduction of the labor force in Latin America. Particular emphasis is given to Mexico.

FASCELL, DANTE, ed. *International News: Freedom under Attack.* London, Sage Publications, 1976, 320 pp. "Freedom of press and the free flow of news and information are under attack around the globe." The authors treat of threats against "one of the world's most fundamental and cherished freedoms."

FISHER, DESMOND. *The Right to Communicate: A Status Report* (Reports and Papers on Mass Communication, no. 94). Paris, UNESCO, 1982, 55 pp. Reviews a number of key concepts associated with the "right to communicate": the information society, freedom of information, the individual and society, etc. Also summarizes major UNESCO meetings on this question.

FISHER, GLEN. *American Communications in a Global Society.* Norwood, N.J. Ablex, 1979, 165 pp. A useful introduction to some recent American thinking on the current world communication debate. Prognosis and prospects for the 1980s.

FRIEDRICH-EBERT-STIFTUNG ORGANIZATION (FES). *Television News in a North-South Perspective.* Bonn. Friedrich-Ebert Stiftung, 1981, 180 pp. The major speeches and presentations made at a seminar on television news in 1981, sponsored by the FES and the Asia-Pacific Broadcasting Union.

GALLAGHER, MARGARET. *Unequal Opportunities: The Case of Women and the Media.* Paris, UNESCO, 1981, 221 pp. Thorough appraisal of the "women and the media" issue, both in developed and developing countries. Extensive documentation and bibliography included.

GANLEY, GLADYS D., and OSWALD H. *To Inform or to Control? The New Communications Networks.* New York, McGraw-Hill, 1982, 250 pp. The emergence of new electronic communications systems and their effects on U.S. domestic industries and developing countries.

GERBNER, GEORGE, and SIEFERT, MARSHA, eds. *World Communication: A Handbook.* New York/London, Longman, 1984, 527 pp. A total of 70 authors, from 25 countries, are represented in this review of global communication issues. The book is divided into five sections: global perspectives on information; transnational communications: the flow of news and images; telecommunications: satellites and computers; mass communications: development within national contexts; intergovernmental systems: toward international policies.

GUBACK, THOMAS. *Notes on Imperialism and the Film Industry.* Urbana, University of Illinois, Institute of Communication Research, 1978, 14 pp. A study of the role of film as a commercial communication medium in regional and international systems of dominance and dependence.

———, and VARIS, TAPIO. *Transnational Communication and Cultural Industries.* (Reports and Papers on Mass Communication, no. 92). Paris, UNESCO, 1982, 55 pp. After attempting to define communication transnationals, the authors provide an overall quantitative survey of the transnational flow of mass media materials, and a study of transnational film and television businesses. Also presents case studies of Thailand and Argentina.

HABERMAN, PETER, and DE FONTGALLAND, GUY. *Development Communications: Rhetoric and Reality.* Singapore, Asian Mass Communication Research and Information Centre, 1978, 192 pp. State-of-the-art presentation on development communications and examination of this concept as it has emerged in Asia during the 1970s.

HACHTEN, WILLIAM A. *The World News Prism: Changing Media, Clashing Ideologies.* Ames, Iowa State University Press, 1981, 133 pp. Overview of the development of international communication technology since the end of the Second World War. Basically Western perspectives on political, ideological, economic, and geographic factors inhibiting the flow of international news.

HAMELINK, CEES. *The Corporate Village: The Role of Transnational Corporations in International Communications.* Rome, IDOC International, 1977, 233 pp. A well-documented study of global ownership of the electronics, broadcasting, newspaper, and publishing industries. Views international communications as part of the political and economic patterns of the world, supporting one-way traffic from rich to poor countries.

———. *Cultural Autonomy in Global Communications: Planning National Information Policy.* New York, Longman, 1982, 160 pp. Analysis of Western perceptions of Third World initiatives in the communications field; cultural dependency vs. autonomous development; reappraisals of current development models; the future of global information networks.

———. *Finance and Information.* Norwood, N.J., Ablex, 1982, 192 pp. Implications of converging interests between information and financial sectors are discussed in view of the need for NWICO.

———. *Transnational Data Flow in the Information Age.* Lund, Studentlitterature AB/Chartwell Bratt, Ltd., 1984, 115 pp. The author's point of departure is that the "information age" will demand the establishment of the primacy of private technology. Hamelink warns that if critical decision-making in the area of telematics technology is left to private interests, the unequal distribution of vital resources will be further aggravated.

HARMS, LEROY STANLEY, and RICHSTAD, JIM, eds. *Evolving Perspectives on the Right to Communicate.* Honolulu, East-West Communications Institute, 1977, 285 pp. Twenty-two original essays examining the "right to communicate" from various cultural and ideological viewpoints.

HARRIS, PHIL. *Reporting Southern Africa: Western News Agencies Reporting from Southern Africa.* Paris, UNESCO, 1981, 168 pp. First part of the text treats historical role of Western news agencies in spread of colonialism. The author then examines systems of media control in South Africa and Zimbabwe, including content analysis of news-agency stories.

———; MALCZEK, HARALD; AND OZKÖK, ERTUGRUL. *Flow of News in the Gulf*. (New Communication Order Series, no. 3). Paris, UNESCO, 1979/80, 65 pp. Examines the content and volume of news exchanged between the Gulf region and Europe. One basic conclusion points to a "correlation between the volume of news transmitted on a given country and the diplomatic and economic relations this country maintains with the countries in which these agencies are based."

HEACOCK, ROGER. *UNESCO and the Media*. Geneva, Institut Universitaire des Hautes Etudes Internationales, 1977, 62 pp. Political analysis of the controversy surrounding UNESCO media activities, up to and including the 1976 general conference. The San José conference, 1976, is the subject of special study.

HEDEBRO, GÖRAN. *Communication and Social Change in Developing Nations*. Ames, Iowa State University Press, 1982, 142 pp. Analyzes the following aspects of the communication/development debate: communication and the diffusion of innovation; uses of communication for development; flows between countries; alternative uses of communication; new perspectives on development.

HUET, ARMEL; ION, JACQUES; LEFÈBVRE, ALAIN; MIÈGE, BERNARD; and PERON, RENÉ. *Capitalisme et industries culturelles*. Grenoble, Presses Universitaires de Grenoble, 1978, 198 pp. The authors examine the role of the state in promoting/creating new markets for cultural products and activities. Focus on amateur photography, records, and new audio-visual products.

IBRAHIM, SALAH M. *The Flow of International News into Sudan, the Middle East and Africa*. Khartoum, Ministry of Culture and Information, Al Sahafa Press, 1981, 25 pp. Concludes that recent efforts to change direction of international flow of news, as well as distorted coverage of the Third World, have been largely to no avail. Calls for national agencies to professionalize news-gathering activities.

Institut universitaire d'études du développement (IUED). *Les nouvelles chaines. Techniques modernes de télécommunication et tiers-monde: pièges et promesses*. Paris, PUF, 1983. Articles by European, African, and Middle Eastern specialists on the problems linked to the imminent launching of direct broadcast satellites. The overall context is "a redefinition of North/South relations."

Instituto Latinoamericano de Estudios Transnacionales (ILET). *A Survey of the Transnational Structure of the Mass Media and Advertising* (report prepared for the UN Center for Transnational Corporations, New York). Mexico City, ILET, 1978, 350 pp. One of the most complete, thoroughly documented studies thus far carried out on the mass media and the transnational structure; advertising and the transnational structure; advertising and development.

———. *Informes ILET.* Mexico City, ILET, División de Estudios de la Comunicación, 1977, 147 pp. Includes bibliography references, relevant documents (UNESCO recommendations, nonaligned resolutions, etc.), case studies, and complementary texts on the flow of international news.

IWENS, J.L., and VERCRUYSSE, J.P. *Du télégraphe au télétexte: les réseaux du profit.* Paris, Editions Ouvrières, 1982. Within the context of the North/South debate, the authors examine the "privatization" of telecommunication networks, telecommunication transnationals, and their current market strategies.

KASHLEV, YURI. *The Mass Media and International Relations.* Prague, International Organization of Journalists, 1983, 169 pp. Examines, from a Soviet perspective, the following aspects of the mass media and international relations: the communications explosion; information exchange; information imperialism; the struggle for a new information order. He concludes by urging international media to strengthen peace and understanding, and to develop East-West cooperation.

KATZ, ELIHU, and WEDELL, GEORGE. *Broadcasting in the Third World.* Cambridge, Mass., Harvard University Press, 1977, 305 pp. The authors examine radio and television broadcasting in 11 countries of Asia, Africa, and Latin America. Findings confirm that, in general, inherited models are being applied with "too little questioning of their origin or usefulness."

LANISPERO, YRJO; SHAHZADEH, IBRAHIM; and ANG, LUKE. *Television News Exchange in Asia: A Case Study.* Singapore, Asian Mass Communication Research and Information Center (AMIC), 1976, 77 pp. A study focused on the present state of television news; the views of members of the Asian Broadcasting Union on the need for additional newsfilm supply; the existing and planned capabilities of member organizations for newsfilm exchange.

LENT, JOHN. *Topics in Third World Mass Communications,* Hong Kong, Asian Research Service, 1979, 123 pp. Covers four basic areas: how to make mass media economically and culturally practical for developing nations; how the media can serve the masses; the conflict between press freedom and developmental journalism; mass media research.

———, and VILANILAM, JOHN, eds. *The Use of Development News: Case Studies of India, Malaysia, Ghana and Thailand.* Singapore, Asian Mass Communication and Research Information Center, 1979, 110 pp. Content analysis of development information in Asian and African print and broadcast media.

MATTELART, ARMAND. *Multinational Corporations and the Control of Culture: The Ideological Apparatuses of Imperialism.* Atlantic Highlands, N.J./Brighton, Humanities Press/Harvester Press, 1979, 304 pp. A carefully documented study of the cultural penetration of media multinationals in television, publishing, the press, cinema, and leisure and cultural activities.

———. *Transnationals and the Third World: The Struggle for Culture.* South Hadley, Mass., Bergin and Harvey Publishers, 1983, 184 pp. This study, commissioned by the U.N. Center for Transnational Corporations, focuses on the negative socio-cultural impact of transnational firms on developing countries. The author concludes that the international communication debates have placed undue emphasis on news flow, to the detriment of critical examination of communications technology.

———, and MICHÈLE. *De l'usage des médias en temps de crise: les nouveax profils des industries de la culture.* Paris, Alain Moreau, 1979, 448 pp. Presents latest strategies of the cultural industries in response to the economic crisis. Section II, "New Cultural Order," is particularly relevant.

———; DELCOURT, XAVIER, and MATTELART, MICHÈLE. *International Image Markets: In Search of an Alternative Perspective.* London, Comedia, 1985, 180 pp. A provocative study on the audiovisual panorama in the era of the transnationals, with particular reference to the Latin-European dimension. Provides a critique of such standard concepts as "alternative communication," "cultural imperialism," and "South-South cooperation."

———, and SCHMUCLER, HECTOR. *Communication and Information Technologies: Freedom of Choice for Latin America.* Norwood, N.J., Ablex, 1985. Analysis of various authoritarian "computerization models" now in use in Latin America. Advocates different type of North/South cooperation, not based on market mechanism.

———, and SIEGELAUB, SETH, eds. *Communication and Class Struggle. Vol. I. Capitalism, Imperialism.* New York/Bagnolet, France, International General, 1979, 445 pp. First general Marxist anthology of writings on communication, information, and culture. With regard to NWICO, the sections dealing with the following topics are especially relevant: colonialism; the industrialization of communication; the processes of standardization and concentration; the implications of new technology.

MATTELART, MICHÈLE. *Women and the Cultural Industries.* Paris. UNESCO, 1982, 75 pp. Deals with an important aspect of the international communication debates: how women are affected by the cultural industries. Includes discussion of mass culture and social cohesion; the media and women's daily life; the present redefining of moral values brought about by the socioeconomic crisis.

MAYOBRE MACHADO, JOSÉ, *La formulacíon de políticas de comunicación.* Caracas, Ministerio de Información y Turismo, 1979, 31 pp. Discussion of national communication policies in Latin America, viewed as essential step toward achievement of NWICO.

———. *Información, dependencia, y desarrollo: la prensa y el nuevo orden economico internacional.* Caracas, Monte Avila Editores, 1976, 212 pp. One of the first works to relate the New International Economic Order to the press. The author concludes by advocating that the press assume its role as an instrument for change in the Third World.

MCANANY, EMILE G.; SCHNITMAN, JORGE; and JANUS, NOREEN, eds. *Commu-*

nication and Social Structure: Critical Studies in Mass Media Research. New York/Eastbourne, Praeger/Holt-Saunders, 1981, 341 pp. Anthology of articles focusing on social structures, social change, and their relationship to mass communications. Provides an excellent up-to-date survey of the current state of critical communications research.

MCPHAIL, THOMAS L. *Electronic Colonialism: The Future of International Broadcasting and Communications.* Beverly Hills, Calif., Sage Publications, 1981, 259 pp. Account of both Western and Third World positions in the international communication debate. Argues that the future may be defined by further government control of media.

MÉTAYER, GÉRARD. *La société malade de ses communications.* Paris, Bordad, 1980, 223 pp. Sociological analysis, based on economic and political forecasting, of effects of new communication technology on social relations. Calls for more critical appraisal of the "information society" concept.

MITRA ASOK. *Information Imbalance in Asia.* Singapore, Asian Mass Communication Research and Information Centre (AMIC), 1975, 18 pp. Deals with areas of news imbalance: distance between the information multinationals and small nationals; and the opinion-forming sector in Asian countries that seems to be rapidly passing into multinational hands.

MOSCO, VINCENT. *Pushbutton Fantasies: Critical Perspectives on Videotex and Information Technology.* Norwood, N.J., Ablex, 1982, 195 pp. Emphasizes which social groups stand to gain or lose most from growth of information technology, particularly videotex.

MOWLANA, HAMID. *International Flow of Information: A Global Report and Analysis.* Paris, UNESCO (forthcoming). A richly informative study that charts a future course for international communications research. The author describes and evaluates international communications research in four main chapters devoted to news and information flow, radio and tèlevision broadcasting, communication systems and data processing technologies, and the "quintessential international activity: planetary resource information flow."

MURPHY, BRIAN. *The World Wired Up: Unscrambling the New Communications Puzzle.* London, Comedia, 1983, 160 pp. Attempts to demystify the technological aura of the new communication systems with emphasis on satellite broadcasting, cable television, and informatics. The transnational control of world markets for the new technology is also analyzed.

NORDENSTRENG, KAARLE, and SCHILLER, HERBERT, eds. *National Sovereignty and International Communication.* Norwood, N.J., Ablex, 1979, 286 pp. Sixteen articles focusing on information and cultural dependence. Divided into four sections: communication and national development; direct satellite broadcasting; international law; the new global balance.

NORDENSTRENG KAARLE, and VARIS, TAPIO. *TV Traffic—A One-Way Street? A Survey and Analysis of the International Flow of Television Programme Materials.* (Reports and Papers on Mass Communication, no. 70). Paris,

UNESCO, 1974, 62 pp. The well-known study on world production, content, and distribution of television programs. The authors conclude that there is a one-way flow originating in the United States, the United Kingdom, and West Germany.

NOUIRA, HEDI. *Information et communication. Discours consacrés aux problèmes de l'information et de la communication.* Tunis, Secrétariat d'Etat à l'Information, 1978, 106 pp. A collection of speeches on nonaligned positions, Arab broadcasting, and information flow in the Arab countries.

OPUBOR, ALFRED E., and NWUNELI, ONURA, E. *The Development and Growth of the Film Industry in Nigeria.* Lagos, National Council for Arts and Culture, 1979, 119 pp. Deals with the cultural, economic, linguistic, and historical problems related to the creation of an indigenous film industry.

Organization for Economic Cooperation and Development (OECD). *An Exploration of Legal Issues in Information and Communication Technologies.* Paris, OECD, 1983, 151 pp. This text is divided into two sections: legal aspects of information technology; and legal problems posed by Transborder Data Flow. Includes analysis of the free flow of information, freedom of information, and national information sovereignty.

PAZ, IDA. *Medios masivos, ideología y propaganda imperialista* (Cuadernos de la revista Unión). Havana, Unión de Escritores y Artistas de Cuba, 1977, 130 pp. Examines the different formulas and pseudo-cultural approaches that make use of the mass media to reinforce the dominant ideology in a period of crisis.

PIERCE, ROBERT. *Keeping the Flame: Media and Government in Latin America.* New York, Hastings House, 1979, 270 pp. Treats important theme related to debates on NWICO: relations between government and the media. Also analyzes communication systems in 9 Latin American countries.

PORTALES, DIEGO, et al. *Comunicación transnacional: conflicto politico y cultural.* Lima, DESCO/ILET, 1982, 186 pp. Papers relating to the democratization of communication. Subjects treated include communications and transnational culture; new communication technology and alternative communications.

The Public Agenda Foundation. *The Speaker and the Listener: A Public Perspective on Freedom of Expression.* New York, 1980, 67 pp. The results of a major public opinion survey in the United States, shedding light on one of the main issues discussed in connection with NWICO: government control of the media. The survey shows that public opinion, in sharp contrast to media leaders, overwhelmingly favors government intervention in the media in order to guarantee fairness and equal coverage of all issues.

QUENNEY, KATHYRN. *Direct Broadcast Satellites and the United Nations.* Aan der Rijn, Sijthoff, Noordhoff, 1978, 327 pp. An in-depth study of the economic, legal, technical, and socio-cultural implications of direct broadcast satellites. Principal sources used are United Nations meetings, records, and reports.

RACHTY, GEHAN, and SABAT, KHALIL. *Importation of Films for Cinema and Television in Egypt.* (Communication and Society Series, no. 7). Paris, UNESCO, 1980, 78 pp. This study shows that Egypt "is heavily dependent on a small number of foreign companies, based in a few industrialized countries, which supply most of the films for cinema and television programming."

RADA, JUAN. *Problemas y posibilidades de la actual revolución informativa.* Mexico City, ILET, 1980, 55 pp. Examines how control of computer technology by industrialized countries affects the Third World, particularly in terms of the international division of labor.

RASKIN, A.H. *Report on News Coverage of Belgrade UNESCO Conference.* New York, The National News Council, 1981, 16 pp. Study of American media coverage of 1980 Belgrade UNESCO general conference. Concludes that "news analysis and feature stories concentrated almost exclusively on Western worries about UNESCO initiatives, with little presentation of opposing viewpoints."

READ, WILLIAM. *America's Mass Media Merchants.* Baltimore, Johns Hopkins University Press, 1976, 209 pp. Examines the predominance of American mass media in the global transfer of information and entertainment. The author defends the position that "information sovereignty" is an unacceptable alternative to the "free flow" principle.

REYES MATTA, FERNANDO. *La comunicación alternativa como respuesta democrática.* Mexico City, ILET, 1981, 27 pp. Presents ILET conception of "alternative communication." Also demystifies current communication slogans such as the "demassification of the media."

RICHSTAD, JIM, and ANDERSON, MICHAEL H., eds. *Crisis in International News Policies and Prospects.* New York, Columbia University Press, 1981, 473 pp. Series of articles by some of the most important proponents of NWICO. Basically oriented toward the news question.

ROBINSON, GERTRUDE JOCH. *News Agencies and World News in Canada, the United States and Yugoslavia: Methods and Data.* Fribourg, Switzerland, University Press of Fribourg, 1981, 227 pp. Examines Tanjung, the Yugoslav news agency; news flow; Canadian press coverage of international events. Also provides a general analysis of the NWICO debates.

RONCAGLIOLO, RAFAEL; JANUS, NOREEN; and PORTALES, DIEGO. *Publicidad, economía y democratización de las comunicaciones.* Mexico City, ILET, 1981, 20 pp. Overall analysis of communication and democracy, with particular reference to advertising in Latin America.

SCHILLER, DANIEL. *Telematics and Government.* Norwood, N.J., Ablex, 1982, 256 pp. Systematic assessment of the role of government in computerization in U.S. and other societies.

SCHILLER, HERBERT. *Communication and Cultural Domination.* White Plains, N.Y., International Arts and Sciences Press, 1976, 126 pp. Offers a critical appraisal of mass communication systems in the United States. Explains the origin of the "free-flow doctrine" in terms of the rising economic hegemony of the United States after the Second World War.

———. *Information and the Crisis Economy.* Norwood, N.J., Ablex, 1984, 133 pp. Analyzes the way in which information and the new communication technologies are being used to overcome various crises afflicting the United States and other advanced industrial market societies. Democratic participation in decision-making is said to be the paramount issue.

———. *Mass Communication and American Empire.* Boston, Beacon Press, 1971, 170 pp. One of the first works to treat the political and economic aspects of American mass communication structures and policies. Includes proposals for a democratic restructuring of the media.

———. *Who Knows? Information in the Age of the Fortune 500.* Norwood, N.J., Ablex, 1981, 187 pp. Analysis of the political economy of information in the age of the "Fortune 500." Warns that both the New International Economic Order and NWICO can be brought into line with the needs of the transnationals.

SCHMUCLER, HECTOR. *La sociedad informatizada y las perspectivas de la democracía.* Mexico City, ILET, 1981, 17 pp. Sociological analysis of the incompatibility between the "computer society" and democracy. Particular reference is made to Latin America.

SCHNITMAN, JORGE A. *Film Industries in Latin America: Dependency and Development.* Norwood, N.J., Ablex, 1983. Comprehensive view of interrelated development of international and domestic film industries in developing countries. Also discusses the advantages and disadvantages of state protectionism.

SCHRAMM, WILBUR, and ATWOOD, ERWIN. *Circulation of News in the Third World: A Study of Asia.* Hong Kong, The Chinese University Press, 1981, 352 pp. Relates to one of the earliest issues involved in the NWICO debates: news flow into and out of Third World countries. Schramm and Atwood challenge the argument that transnational news agencies devote only 20 to 30 percent of their news coverage (in Asia) to the developing countries.

SIGNITZER, BENNO. *Regulation of Direct Broadcasting from Satellites: The UN Involvement.* New York, Praeger, 1976, 112 pp. Traces the history, up to 1976, of UN involvement in the regulation of direct broadcast satellites. Also analyzes the political and legislative process within the UN Outer Space Committee with particular reference to the positions of member states on the "free-flow doctrine."

SINGHAM, A.W., ed. *The Non-Aligned Movement in World Politics.* Westport, Conn., Lawrence Hill, 1977, 273 pp. Part II of this work, "Non-Alignment and Global Mass Communications," is of particular relevance for the NWICO debates. Includes texts on the mechanisms of cultural imperialism, an Asian view of cultural imperialism, and the need for a news-flow code.

SLACK, JENNIFER DARYL. *Communication Technologies and Society: Conceptions of Casuality and the Politics of Technological Intervention.* Norwood,

N.J. Ablex, 1984, 166 pp. Primarily a critical analysis of the predominant forms of contemporary technological intervention and the conceptions of the relationship between technology and society on which they are based. The author's aim is to develop a theoretical understanding of the relationship between communication technology and society that can form the basis for sound technological criticism and intervention.

———, and FEJES, FRED, eds. *The Ideology of Information.* Norwood, N.J., Ablex (forthcoming). A collection of articles by critical communication researchers on the "information age" concept viewed particularly in terms of its ideological implications.

SMITH, ANTHONY. *The Geopolitics of Information: How Western Culture Dominates the World.* London, Faber and Faber, 1980; 192 pp. One of the most often cited works dealing with communication questions and NWICO. Provides convincing proof of real imbalances in the developing world, and advocates "interdependence" between North and South.

SMYTHE, DALLAS W. *Dependency Road: Communications, Capitalism, Consciousness and Canada.* Norwood, N.J., Ablex, 1981, 347 pp. Deals with Canada's present state of dependence on U.S. communication industries. Also analyzes emergence of the "consciousness industry" in both countries

SOMAVÍA, JUAN. *Democratización de las comunicaciones: una perspective latinoamericana.* Mexico City, ILET. 1979, 53 pp. The democratization of communication is studied in opposition to control of communication systems by the transnationals. Proposes alternative development strategies.

SUSSMAN, LEONARD. *Mass News Media and the Third World Challenge.* Beverly Hills, Calif./London, Sage Publications, 1977, 80 pp. One of the major Western spokesmen on NWICO presents the "government-control" argument as the paramount issue. Within this context, Sussman examines the main UNESCO meetings on communication up to 1977.

TEHRANIAN, MAJID; HAKIMZADEH, FARHAD; and VIDALE, MARCELLOL. *Communications Policy for National Development: A Comparative Perspective.* Tehran, Iran Communications and Development Institute, 1977, 461 pp. Texts by international specialists focusing on the use of communications to assist development. Case-studies of Benin, Brazil, India, and the Islamic Republic of Iran.

THIAM, THIERNO-DJIBI. *Les flux de l'information sud-sud en Afrique noire.* Fribourg, Editions Universitaires Fribourg, 1982, 178 pp. A study of South-South information flow in black Africa. Also analyzes modern communications technology in traditional African societies.

TUNSTALL, JEREMY. *The Media Are American: Anglo-American Media in the World.* London, Constable, 1977, 352 pp. An in-depth historical summary of the global influence of American and British media and media patterns.

TURN, REIN, ed. *Transborder Data Flows: Concerns in Privacy Protection and Free Flow of Information.* Washington, D.C., American Federation of Information Processing Societies, 1979, 2 vols. Compilation of present positions and considerations related to transborder data flow. Also details relevant primary legislation in major Western countries.

UNESCO, *Cultural Industries: A Challenge for the Future of Culture.* Paris, UNESCO, 1982, 236 pp. A collection of texts by specialists representing varying viewpoints on a number of aspects of the cultural-industries question: concentration and internationalization, the role of government, effects on women, etc.

VAN AERNSBERGEN, JACQUES; TONNAER, CLEMENT; and VAN DER VEEN, HANS. *Inter-Press Service: News from the Third World.* Nijmegen, University of Nijmegen, 1979, 91 pp. Thorough examination of IPS, viewed as an alternative information structure. Also presents the new conception of information advanced by IPS.

VANDINH, TRANH. *Independence, Liberation, Revolution.* Norwood, N.J., Ablex (forthcoming). A comprehensive study of the Third World, based on three historical currents: independence, liberation, and revolution. The struggle of the Third World of a New International Economic Order and a New World Information Order is viewed as interrelated with and parallel to struggles in the capitalist and socialist worlds.

VARIS, TAPIO. *The Impact of Transnational Corporations on Communication.* Tampere, Tampere Peace Research Institute, 1975. 58 pp. Views the "transnationalization" of communication media as basic support for the international movements of capital. Includes a case-study of the Phillips Corporation.

WICKLEIN, JOHN. *Electronic Nightmare: The New Communications and Freedom.* New York, Viking Press, 1981, 282 pp. Asks a key question relating to new communication technology: Who will control the systems? Examines both benefits and risks for individual liberties.

DOCUMENTS, PERIODICALS, ARTICLES

ALI, S.M. DEPTHNEWS. "A Model for a Third World Feature Agency." Paper commissioned by the Edmund R. Murrow Center of the Fletcher School of Law and Diplomacy, for its conference on the Third World and press freedom, New York, May 11–13, 1977, 9 pp. Examines how Depth-news Service in Asia evolved as an attempt to increase the flow of information from Asia to the West.

AMUNUGAMA, SARATH. "Communication Issues Confronting the Developing Nations" in George Gerbner and Marsha Siefert, eds., *World Communications: A Handbook,* New York/London, Longman, 1948, pp. 56–62. Examines the following issues facing developing countries: the impact of modern media on traditional cultures; the need for a free and balanced information flow; technology transfer. Although acknowledging the need for the latest media technology in the developing world, Amunugama also holds that priority should be given to the attainment of socially desirable ends.

———. "Text and Context in Communications Research in Asia," in Sarath Amunugama and Abdul Rahman b Mohd Said, eds., *Communication Research in Asia,* Singapore, Asian Mass Communication Research Information Centre, 1982, pp. 28–49. Critique of dominant communication theories as applied to Asia. Advocates "participatory" community communication models.

BECKER, JÖRG. "L'Europe et le Tiers Monde dans la bataille de l'information," *Le Monde Diplomatique,* Paris, January 1982. Argues convincingly that, in many respects, Western Europe, like much of the Third World, is now in a position of information dependency vis-à-vis the United States. Provides evidence that the North/South dividing line applied to communication issues is no longer valid.

BIELENSTEIN, DIETER, ed. *Towards a New World Information Order: Consequences for Development Policy.* Bonn, Institute for International Relations/Friedrich-Ebert-Stiftung, 1979, 119 pp. The report of a conference on NWICO held in Bonn, December 1978. The conference attempted to draw practical conclusions for development cooperation between developed and developing countries.

BOLLA, GÉRARD. "What the Third World Wants, As Seen by the Third World," in *Communications in a Changing World.* Washington, D.C., The Media Institute, 1983, pp. 10–15. Speech presented at a conference sponsored by the Media Institute in 1982. Offers latest UNESCO position on developments concerning NWICO, with specific reference to the "government-control" argument.

Commission of the U.S.S.R. for UNESCO. *Bulletin* 3/57/1984. Moscow, Novosti Press Agency Publishing House, 1984, 48 pp. Articles on the Soviet position on international communication issues, including TASS and international cooperation; Soviet Radio and TV vis-à-vis international exchanges of information; international legal aspects of the new order.

Communication Research in Third World Realities. The Hague, Institute of Social Studies, 1980, 42 pp. Report of a policy workshop on the state-of-the-art in communication research. A series of recommendations are offered for changing the status quo.

Communications in a Changing World. (vol. 2, *Issues in International Information*), Washington, D.C., The Media Institute, 1983, 71 pp. Papers presented at an international conference on the media question held in 1982. Deals with the position of UNESCO, government involvement in communications, advertising, and a number of other issues.

Development Dialogue: Towards a New World Information and Communication Order. Uppsala, Sweden, 1981, 172 pp. Special issue devoted to various subjects involved in the call for NWICO: the democratization of communication, the microelectronics revolution, the right to inform.

Documents presented to the International Commission for the Study of Communication Problems. (MacBride Commission), Paris, UNESCO, 1977.

Over 100 documents written by international specialists on major aspects of the world communications debate.

FARAONE, ROQUE. *La reproduction idéologique dans les informations internationales: des exemples de l'AFP.* Paper presented at the general assembly of the International Association of Mass Communication Research (IAMCR), Paris, September 6-10, 1982, 20 pp. Examines ideological reproduction inherent in international news, through case-study of Agence France Presse. Concludes that information depends on market mechanisms, political limitations, and professional ideology.

FEJES, FRED. "Media Imperialism: An Assessment," *Media Culture and Society,* London, no. 3, 1981, pp. 281-89. Important review of the "media imperialism" thesis, as it has developed since the 1970s. Calls for more coherent concern for "wider theoretical issues."

Freedomways: Quarterly Review of Freedom Movement, New York, vol. 22, no. 3, 1982, 209 pp. (theme: "The Information Century"). Offers Third World perspective on a new order. Particularly interesting articles: "A Palestinian Perspective on the New Information Order" and "The Caribbean: National Values and the Information Flow."

GONZALES MANET, ENRIQUE. "Medios de difusión, cultura y cambio social en América Latina," *Boletin UNESCO,* Paris, July-December 1980, pp. 16-28. Examines the development of technology in capitalist countries and its implications for the developing world, particularly Latin America.

HAIGHT, TIMOTHY. "The New American Information Order," in Vincent Mosco and Janet Wasko, eds. *The Critical Communications Review,* Vol. 2, *Changing Patterns of Communications Control,* Norwood, N.J., Ablex, 1984, pp. 101-17. The premise of the article is that the structure of media hegemony within the United States is similar to its international form. Examines the questions, whether American media reform groups can be of assistance in achieving NWICO.

HAMELINK, CEES, ed. *Communication in the Eighties: A Reader on the MacBride Report.* Rome, IDOC International 1980, 62 pp. Critical examination by renowned international specialists of the MacBride Report, viewed within the context of an international environment characterized by "rapid technological change, arms races, and economic recession in industrial market-economies, on one hand, and growing power for transnational industrial conglomerates, on the other hand."

HORTON, PHILIP, ed. *The Third World and Press Freedom.* London, Praeger, 1978, 253 pp. The papers of an international conference on press freedom, held in New York in 1977. News flow in the Third World; international legal aspects of freedom of information; developmental journalism.

Informing a Global Society. Corvallis, Oregon State University, 1981, 90 pp. Papers presented at a conference on international communications sponsored by the Press Club of San Francisco, April 1981.

International IDOC Bulletin, New Series, Rome, International Documentation and Communication Center, no. 4–5, April-May 1980 (theme: "The New International Information Order"). "Alternative Communications"; "The Alternative Press in Mozambique"; "The Chilean Review APSI"; "Low-Cost Documentation Systems and Techniques."

Journal of Communication. Philadelphia, vol. 28, no. 4. autumn 1978 (theme: "The Great Debate begins"). Articles deal with news flow, the nonaligned news pool, and computer systems.

———, vol. 29, no. 2, spring 1979 (theme: "International Information: A New Order"). Includes articles on international and local coverage of Third World events, development news, information sovereignty, and reactions to the UNESCO Mass Media Declaration.

———, vol. 29, no. 3, summer 1979 (theme: "Transborder Data Flow: New Frontiers or None?"). Deals with movement of data on business and private affairs across national boundaries via computer-satellite links. Contributors focus on concerns of the developing world vis-à-vis the invasion of privacy and the degree of political and economic control exercised by the multinationals.

———, vol. 31, no. 4, autumn 1981 (theme: "The Press, the US and UNESCO"). Articles are primarily devoted to the MacBride Report and Western press coverage of the 1980 UNESCO general conference.

———, vol. 32, no. 3, summer 1982 (theme: "IPDC in Mexico: US-UNESCO Turning Point?"). Three authors analyze various aspects of the IPDC: criticism of U.S. policy, positive U.S. appraisal, and Mexican and U.S. press coverage of the second session of the IPDC council, held in January 1982.

———, winter 1984/85 (forthcoming) (theme: "World Forum of Views on the U.S. Decision to Withdraw from UNESCO"). Special symposium presented with views of major Western, socialist, and Third World scholars and journalists on the role the NWICO debates played in the announced U.S. decision to withdraw from UNESCO.

Journal of International Affairs, New York, Columbia University, vol. 35, no. 2, fall/winter 1981/82, 291 pp. (theme: "Towards a New World Information Order"). Special issue entirely devoted to NWICO debates. Noteworthy for presentation of viewpoints of Western, socialist, and Third World representatives.

KANDIL, HAMDY. "Developing Countries and the New Order in the Field of Information," *The Democratic Journalist,* Prague, no. 2, 1980, pp. 8–11. Details UNESCO information activities. Discusses Western and Third World positions on NWICO.

———. "Statement at the Twenty-Fourth Annual Meeting of the Canadian Commission for UNESCO on 'A New World Information and Communication Order,' " Ottawa, April 21, 1982, 7 pp. Summarizes recent UNESCO positions on various questions, including: protection of journalists; the right to communicate; new communication technology.

MACBRIDE, SEÁN. *"The Protection of Journalists,"* document presented to the International Commission for the Study of Communication Problems (Document no. 90). Paris, UNESCO, 1977, 30 pp. plus appendices. The head of the commission here presents his views on one of the more controversial issues discussed in relation to NWICO.

MASMOUDI, MUSTAPHA. "The New World Information Order," document presented to the International Commission for the Study of Communication Problems (Document no. 31), Paris, UNESCO, 1978, 24 pp. One of the major NWICO spokesmen presents some key issues that fuelled the early debates: the concept of information as a social good; sovereign rights of states; self-reliance; New International Economic Order.

M'BOW, AMADOU-MAHTAR. "Address at the Opening of the Conference of Journalists of Non-Aligned Countries on the Media (NAMEDIA)," New Delhi, December 1984 (UNESCO Document DG/83/49), 4 pp. In addition to outlining the high points of the communications debate, the director-general of UNESCO states that this new order is becoming an "established fact." In his opinion, this position is justified by the current technological revolution and by the fact that in the North and the South, peoples are determined to assert their national and cultural identity.

———. "Lecture on UNESCO's Role in the Establishment of a New World Information and Communication Order," Lagos, Institute of International Affairs, January 1984 (UNESCO Document DG/84/5), 6 pp. High points of the debate on NWICO as of 1976. Emphasizes the latest activities of the International Programme for the Development of Communication (IPDC).

"Media Development," *Journal of the World Association for Christian Communication,* London, vol. 27, no. 4, 1980 (theme: "Towards a New International Information Order"). Entire issue is devoted to theme of the new order, with articles by leading representatives on various aspects of the debate: national communication policies; the role of the churches; communication technology; communication research.

MOWLANA, HAMID. "Technology Versus Revolution: Communications in the Iranian Revolution," *Journal of Communication,* vol. 29, no. 3, summer 1979, pp. 107–12. Analyzes the role of traditional media in the process of revolutionary change. Necessary perspective for evaluating introduction of communication technology in developing countries.

NACLA Report on the Americas. New York, North American Congress on Latin America, vol. 16, no. 4, July–August 1982, 46 pp. (theme: "Towards a New Information Order"). Progressive American view supporting goals of a new order both abroad and at home. Articles cover old information order and proposals for a new order.

PASQUALI, ANTONIO. "Contradiccíon entre libertad y equilibrio informativo?" *Chasqui: Revista Latinoamericana de Comunicación,* Quito, October–December 1983, pp. 26–31. Philosophical essay demonstrating that there is no contradiction between the development of communication and the free flow of information. Sustains that first priority should always be given to rights of media users.

PASQUINI, JOSÉ M. "Agencias noticias alternativas en América Latina," *Chasqui: Revista Latinoamericana de Comunicación,* Quito, October-December 1981, pp. 36–41. Critical perspective on "alternative" communications as the concept has been applied in Latin America. Calls for government involvement in truly alternative media projects.

RENAUD, JEAN-LUC. "A Revised Agenda for the New World Information Order: The Transborder Data Flow Issue," *Gazette,* Amsterdam, vol. 34, no. 2, 1984, pp. 117–35. Examines the transborder data-flow question within the context of the NWICO debates. Also includes discussion of NWICO in relation to the New International Economic Order.

ROACH, COLLEEN. "French Press Coverage of the Belgrade UNESCO Conference," *Journal of Communication,* Philadelphia, vol. 31, no. 4, autumn 1981, pp. 175–87. Content analysis of how the French press covered communication issues at the 21st session of the general conference of UNESCO in Belgrade, 1980. Concludes that "only one side of the New Information Order story is being told."

———. "Mexican and U.S. News Coverage of the IPDC at Acapulco," *Journal of Communication,* vol. 32, no. 3, summer 1982, pp. 71–85. Content analysis of American and Mexican press coverage of 2nd council meeting of the IPDC (Acapulco, January 1982). Study shows that the "free flow" question is still a paramount issue for both developing and industrialized countries.

SCHENKEL, PETER. "La estructura de poder de los medios de comunicación en cinco paises latinoamericanos," in Peter Schenkel and Marco Ordonez, eds. *Comunicación y cambio social,* Quito, CIESPAL, 1981, pp. 15–22. Includes five studies on media ownership, the relationship between media owners and political power, and means of production, in Argentina, Chile, Colombia, Mexico, and Peru. Proves interdependence between social communication and social and economic structures.

SUSSMAN, LEONARD. "UNESCO and the U.S. Ultimatum," *Freedom at Issue,* New York, no. 79, July–August 1984, pp. 21–31. Testimony of the executive director of Freedom House at congressional hearings (April 1984) on the announced withdrawal of the United States from UNESCO. Although critical of certain UNESCO policies, Sussman advocates "a course that maintains pressure while avoiding ultimate withdrawal."

SZECSKÖ, TAMAS. "Broadening Lasswell's Paradigm," in Cees Hamelink, ed. *Communication in the Eighties: A Reader on the MacBride Report,* Rome, IDOC International, 1980, pp. 17–22. Finds that the MacBride Report is "the first international document that provides a really global view on the world's communication problems." Also criticizes the report for its treatment of technology, its emphasis on news flow, and its hesitancy with respect to national communication policies.

———. "The Grammar of Global Communications," *The Democratic Journalist,* Prague, no. 1, 1983, pp. 12-18. Analysis of new communication technology in its historical context. Develops thesis in favor of an "organic model" linking the concepts of information and communication.

TOPUZ, HIFZI. "The Disequilibrium of Information," *The Democratic Journalist,* no. 7-8, 1978, pp. 8-10 (part I); no. 9, 1978, pp. 9-16 (part II). Traces development of communication debates within UNESCO from 1970 to 1978. Excellent summary of major events by "inside observer."

———. "The News Agencies Pool of the Non-Aligned Countries," paper presented at UNESCO Meeting of Experts on Development of News Agencies in Asia, Colombo, December 5-9, 1977, 7 pp. History, objectives, and functioning of Non-Aligned news agency pool. Also discusses criticism and problems.

The UNESCO Courier, Paris, UNESCO, April 1977, 34 pp. (theme: "A World Debate on Information: Flood Tide or Balanced Flow?"). Most of the articles deal with various positions on the "free flow of information"—of special interest because texts present the viewpoints of UNESCO officials, representatives of Western and socialist countries, and of the Non-Aligned movement.

———. March 1983, 34 pp. (theme: "Communications"). Latest information on a variety of themes: the UNESCO communication program; world communication year; computers; communication technology; the International Program for the Development of Communication (IPDC).

United States Congress, House of Representatives, Committee on Foreign Affairs, Subcommittee on International Operations. *The WARC and International Communication Policy.* Washington, D.C., United States Government Printing Office, 1980, 122 pp. (96th Congress). Hearings on American proposals and policies for the 1979 World Administrative Radio Conference. Includes speeches of major policy-makers and summary of commentary of the U.S. delegation to the conference.

———, Subcommittee on International Operations and on Human Rights and on International Organizations. *Review of U.S. Participation in UNESCO.* Washington, D.C., United States Government Printing Office, 1982, 287 pp. (97th Congress). Major purpose of the hearings was to determine "whether or not UNESCO had taken any decisions to license journalists or regulate the press" and to examine Third World complaints about the present communication order.

———, Subcommittee on International Organizations. *UNESCO and Freedom of Information.* Washington, D.C., United States Government Printing Office, 1979, 69 pp. (96th Congress). Examines the American perspective on major issues involved in NWICO, particularly in relation to the 1978 general conference of UNESCO (during which the UNESCO Declaration on the Mass Media was adopted).

———, Committee on Government Operations. *International Information*

Flow: Forging a New Framework. Washington, D.C., United States Government Printing Office, 1980, 61 pp. (96th Congress). Analysis of what the information sector now represents in the American economy. Present perils for American economy posed by government regulation of the international flow of information.

United States Department of Commerce. *The Foundations of U.S. Information Policy.* Washington, D.C., National Telecommunications and Information Administration, 1980, 15 pp. United States government submission to high-level OECD conference on information, computers, and communication policy. Focuses on American deliberations on international information policies.

———, National Telecommunications and Information Administration. *Long Range Goals in International Telecommunications and Information: An Outline of United States Policy.* Washington, D.C., Senate Committee on Commerce, Science, and Transportation, 1982. 244 pp. The stated purpose of this report is "to provide a comprehensive delineation of the goals, policies, strategies, and principal issues in the international telecommunications and information field in order to improve the formulation and execution of government policy." Includes survey of public laws dating back to 1979.

VARIS, TAPIO. "The Active Role of Communication in International Relations," paper presented at the Ninth Nordic Peace Research Conference, Oslo, November 12–14, 1982, 11 pp. Examines the role of communication and culture in international relations, particularly within the framework of U.N. and UNESCO activities.

VIERA-GALLO, JOSÉ ANTONIO. "Documentation and the Democratization of Information," *International Social Science Journal,* Paris, UNESCO, vol. 34, no. 4 (94), 1982, pp. 737–46. Deals with rarely studied aspect of a new order: documentation. Excellent analysis of information and documentation systems, especially data banks.

"Voices of Freedom: A World Conference of Independent News Media." Talloires, France, May 15–17, 1981, 74 pp. (working papers). Articles by major Western representatives on political issues relating to a new order, the 1980 general conference of UNESCO, freedom of the press and democracy, and the IPDC. Includes the "Declaration of Talloires."

BIBLIOGRAPHIES

LENT, JOHN. *The New World and International Information Order.* Singapore, Asian Mass Communication Research and Information Centre, 1982, 103 pp.

MOWLANA, HAMID, ed. *The International Flow of News: An Annotated Bibliography.* Paris, UNESCO (forthcoming).

RICHSTAD, JIM, and BOWEN, JACKIE, eds. *International Communication Pol-*

icy and Flow: A Selected Annotated Bibliography. Honolulu, East-West Center and East-West Communication Institute, 1976, 103 pp.

UNESCO Communication Documentation Center. *A New World Information and Communication Order: Towards a Wider and Better Balanced Flow of Information.* Paris, UNESCO, part I, 1979, 73 pp.; part II, 1980–81, 46 pp.

Contributors

Philip Lee studied modern languages at the University of Warwick, England, and conducted at the Royal Academy of Music, London. In 1976 he joined the staff of the World Association for Christian Communication where he is deputy editor of the journal *Media Development*. His spare-time activities still include orchestral and operatic conducting.

Michael Traber is a member of the Swiss Foreign Mission Society. He studied communications at Fordham University and New York University (Ph. D.). He worked as an editor and publisher in Zimbabwe for ten years, and as a teacher of journalism at the All Africa Literature Centre, Kitwe, Zambia. He has written several books in German on Africa and issues of racism. He is currently director of information and interpretation with the World Association for Christian Communication, London.

Washington Uranga is a Latin American journalist and President of UNDA Latin America.

Paul A.V. Ansah studied at the University of Ghana and the University of Bordeaux before graduating B.A. (Hons.) in French from the University of London. Graduate studies in French language and literature took him to the Sorbonne, Paris (M.A. in French), and back to the University of London (Ph. D.). In 1974 he went to the University of Wisconsin to study journalism and Communication (M.A.). He was senior lecturer in French language and literature at the University of Ghana from 1964 to 1974, and senior lecturer and acting director of the School of Journalism and Communication, University of Ghana, from 1975 to 1979. Since 1980 he has been director of the school. He has edited a newspaper and journal in Ghana, written for many academic publications, and conducted communication research in Africa.

Robert A. White studied development sociology and the political economy of Latin America at Cornell University, Ithaca, New York, where his doctoral dissertation was entitled *Structural Factors in Rural Development: The Church and the Peasant in Honduras*. From 1975 to 1978 he was an associate of the Instituto de Investigaciones Socio-Economicas in Tegucigalpa, Honduras, and worked with the Comisión Nacional de Pastoral of the Catholic Church in Honduras. He has also done research on peasant movements in Latin America, and on the use of radio and radio schools for social development. His publications include *Mexico: the Zapata*

Movement and the Revolution; Campesino Movements in Latin America; An Alternative Model of Basic Education; Radio Santa María; Educación Básica y Cambio Estructural. He is research director at the Center for the Study of Communication and Culture, London, established by the Jesuits in 1977.

Gaston Roberge is a Canadian Jesuit priest working in Calcutta, India, where he is director of St. Xavier's College and of Chitrabani, a center for training and experimenting in the use of media for education. He studied at the University of California (M.A. in theater arts) and is the author of *Chitra Bani: A Book on Film Appreciation* (1974); *Films for an Ecology of Mind* (1978); *Mediation: The Action of the Media in our Society* (1978).

Margaret Gallagher studied at the University of London and at the Center for Mass Communication Research, University of Leicester, England. She worked for the BBC before moving to the British Open University where she was deputy head of the Audio Visual Media Research Group. Since 1980 she has researched and developed international projects in the field of women and communication. She is visiting research fellow at the City University, London, where she directs a project on women and television for the Commission of the European Communities.

Johan Galtung is an honorary professor of the Free University, Berlin, and of the University of Alicante, Spain. He is a member of the International Association for Mass Communication Research, and has accepted appointment as professor and rector at the Université Nouvelle Transnationale, Paris.

Herbert I. Schiller is professor of communications at the University of California, San Diego. He is vice-president of the International Association of Mass Communication Research and a trustee of the International Institute of Communications. His many publications include *Mass Communications and American Empire* (1969); *Communication and Cultural Domination* (1976); *Who Knows: Information in the Age of the Fortune 500* (1981).

Colleen Roach is an American communications researcher and writer living in Paris. She studied at the University of Michigan (B.A.), the University of Paris (M.A.) and at the Institut des Hautes Etudes de l'Amérique Latine. Since 1982 she has been in charge of various projects relating to the international communications debate. She is a member of the International Association for Mass Communication Research.

Other Orbis Titles . . .

CONVICTIONS
Political Prisoners—Their Stories
by Arthur Dobrin, Lyn Dobrin, and Thomas F. Liotti
Vivid accounts of the experiences of political prisoners in nine different countries—Argentina, Uganda, Rhodesia/Zimbabwe, Cambodia/Kampuchea, the United States, Poland, the Soviet Union, the Philippines, and Chile.

"Torture, unjust imprisonment, and political repression seem almost commonplace today. In this book the true stories of persons who have gone through such fires remind us of brutal facts that must never be commonplace to any of us. If God is on the side of the oppressed and the sinned against we must listen carefully to their experience—as we can in this little volume—not to recoil in horror but to commit ourselves in solidarity to the many who even now anonymously suffer these same indignities."
Eugene L. Stockwell,
Associate General Secretary,
National Council of Churches

no. 089-X   100pp. pbk. $5.95

HUMAN RIGHTS
A Dialogue Between the First and Third Worlds
by Robert and Alice Evans
A collection of eight case studies of Christians faced with dilemmas involving the violation and/or preservation of basic human rights. The dilemmas involve a variety of issues such as racism, foreign investments by multinational corporations, migrant rights, and housing. Each case study is supplemented by a "teaching note" and by two or three commentaries by well known theologians including Rubem Alves, John Mbiti, Jürgen Moltmann, and Kosuke Koyama.
no. 194-2   236pp. pbk. $9.95

FAMINE
edited by Kevin M. Cahill, M.D.
According to Kevin Cahill, a physician with long experience in Africa, more people will die of famine in this era than in any other period of recorded history. In *Famine*, 13 economists, historians, physicians, and administrators of government and voluntary agencies begin with the premise that this reality is avoidable. They explain the complex causes of hunger and our failure to end it and

they propose practical solutions to the political and technological problem of starvation.

"If you have time to read only one book on famine, this should be it."
The Review of Books and Religion

Kevin Cahill is Director of the Tropical Disease Center of Lenox Hill Hospital in New York City.

no. 132-2　　　　　　　　　　160pp. pbk.　　　　　　　　　　$8.95

FOLLOWING CHRIST IN A CONSUMER SOCIETY
The Spirituality of Cultural Resistance
by John Francis Kavanaugh

"Kavanaugh succeeds in combining a sharp and uncompromising analysis of our contemporary consumer culture with gentle, compassionate and hope-filled reflection on the power of Gospel to transform our cluttered lives. For the social activists who have lost confidence in the spiritual wellsprings of their activism, and for those who do not see the connections between their religious faith and economic and political issues, the author offers new confidence in inescapable connections."
Alternatives

John Kavanaugh, a Jesuit priest and associate professor of philosophy at St. Louis University, is Assistant for Social Ministries of the Jesuit Missouri Province.

no. 090-3　　　　　　　　　　186pp. pbk.　　　　　　　　　　$6.95

JUSTICE AND PEACE EDUCATION
Models for College and University Faculty
edited by David M. Johnson

A collection of models for integrating justice and peace concerns into courses in various disciplines ranging from the humanities, the social sciences, and interdisciplinary studies to business, management, and engineering. Based on the practical educational and research experience of professors in U.S. Catholic colleges and universities, each model includes a course syllabus, a list of required texts for students, and suggested readings for faculty. The result is an intelligent, pragmatic manual for educators seeking to promote a more just and peaceful world. Contributors include Monika Hellwig, William Byron, David O'Brien, Marie Augusta Neal, Thomas Shannon, and Suzanne Toton.

"A remarkable array of authors and a really sophisticated approach in which peace and justice themes are introduced without despoiling the inner integrity of the various disciplines."
Padraic O'Hare,
Boston College

". . . should be a standard resource for all who seek to introduce peace studies into higher eductation."
Betty Reardon, Teachers College,
Columbia University

no. 247-7　　　　　　　　　　256pp. pbk.　　　　　　　　　　$16.95